Published by

One Rib Publications
P. O. Box CB-11968
Nassau, Bahamas
Tel.: (242) 322-5281
Email: onerib@batelnet.bs
or onerib12@hotmail.com

Warning:
No part of this book may be quoted, reproduced, stored in a retrieval system, or transmitted by any means without the written permission of the author. Further, this book or portions thereof, may not be used as text for training, classes, radio broadcast series, as references in other publications, in newspaper/magazine publication(s), speaker series or in any other public manner or forum, whether income generating or otherwise, without the specific written permission of the author.

ISBN: 1-56229-815-1
First published June, 2010

Contents

INTRODUCTION

To write this book was difficult and easy at the same time. It's hard to write about my own life when I look back and see how I wasted time living a life that was leading to nowhere. It's hard to look back and see your friends dying; some literally through drugs or violence and others who are dying because they are not fulfilling their potential.

I think about how painful it was to leave MY 'homeis' behind; the ones I grew up with, played with, used drugs together, partied with, fought together and had many good times. Some of my fondest memories were back on the streets at the famous or infamous "University" of Warren Street, Harlem (Maquay Street), Bain Town, The Valley, Kemp Road and many other "Blocks" as they were called during that time of my life. Today these communities are filled with gangs and gang warfare.

The easy part is when I see the good my life has accomplished and the many people, who have been positively affected by my life story. When I realize the scores of people, young and old, who came to me time and time again and said how their lives were changed by my life testimony and example. Even to this day, more and more people are still coming to me and saying, "Your life story has changed my life. It has caused me to look at my own life." Based upon these sentiments, I have to just go for it and just tell as much as i can that i believe would benefit young people today.

Over and over again people have come to me saying, "Dave, you have to tell your story." There were times when I got tired of telling, tired of re-hashing what had become to me, old stories. I never really looked at my life journey as something that was exciting or important. I never thought of myself as a really bad person; I often thought of other friends and persons I hung around as being bad, but I never thought I was that bad. But I've been reminded over and over that I must tell this story to the youth. Just like the blind man in the Bible who said, "I was blind but now I see." Many are still blind and perhaps what I have to say can open their eyes.

These pages chronicle the life of a young rebel. How I got to be one I don't really know. Sometimes I have no idea why I did some of the things I did but I do know that I was on a mission of destruction until the Day came. If you are a youth, especially those caught up in the "ruff-neck", gangster or thug lifestyle, I trust that as you read, you will see yourself in the mirror and catch yourself in time. If you are not that type of person, I hope this book will help you to never become the way I was.

I dedicate this book to my old gang at the University of Warren Street (UWS) as we used to call it, and to others I hung around with from the many "Blocks". To my old crew including (I use nicknames because in most cases, a nickname was more important than the real name) Knox, Nipper, Bobo, Sasquatch, Boston (deceased), D Count, Pimp Man, 00, Lil Shaft, Priest (deceased), Sir K, Kalix, K Beno, Gregory and Scooby doo Dillet, Rasta, Cheeso (deceased) Boombaclad, Randy, Rudolpho (deceased), Ivy, 'American' Sam, Soup, Duck Quack Sawyer, Science, Mike "Goon" Ramsey, my blood brothers Chimmy B,

Terry B and Congo Bill, I & I, Mash, Chilly, Taps, Pan Brown, Wild Man, Farmer Brown, Bouncer, Psyco, Rev, Donnie G, Doc Sweeting, the gang from Harlem, Kentuck, Kali, Shaft (deceased), Poker, Blood, Santana (deceased), Pirate, Gordo, Don Taylor (deceased), Boom Clark, Rat, and my old friends from all over including Twatus (the Bottom), Keith Wallace (deceased from Black Village), Guff (Farrington Road), 00#2, Fergs and Solid (Valley), Manny (Masons Addition), Skeeter (deceased), Dice (deceased) (Government High), and anyone whom I may have forgotten. I hope some of you or perhaps your children will get a chance to read this book and reflect on the important choices of life. Peace and prayers to those who knew me back then and thought I would be the last one on earth to change. Make that change today while you still have life.

CHAPTER 1

'AN ORDINARY CHILD'

From every indication in my early childhood, it seemed I was destined to be a model citizen; that is, one of those children who makes their parents proud; one, who grows up to be an example in the community. Nothing during my early years seemed to indicate otherwise. I WAS A GOOD BOY.

It has been said that every family has a 'black sheep' and the one in my family who seemed to fit that mould more than any other was my younger brother. As far back as I can remember, "Congo Bill" was the one who was always in trouble. He got whipped so much until we began to think he enjoyed it. I, on the other hand, hardly ever got reprimanded. My older brother was in a different category. He was always mischievous in his own way. He was always popular–a sweet talker, one who everyone liked. He was almost like a con man. He would talk to you real nice, yet he always had something devious somewhere in the back of his mind.

All of my sisters were basically model children. Like my mother, they went to Church and did all the right things. Only one sort of strayed for a while, but even then, she never went far from the pattern set by my mother, who was initially a school teacher and later a housewife. She was always nice although she was tough in her way. She loved her children and always sought the best for them. My father in the early days seemed like the model father and husband; always taking care of the family and giving us the things we needed and desired. A lot of good things happened in my early life, as we seemed to be headed for the typical "Bahamian Dream" or "The American Dream" as its known in the USA.

My father was a member of the Rotary Club and Kiwanis Club, a member of the Bahamas Flying Club, which at that time was an exclusive club for private pilots. In fact he was the first black private pilot in the Bahamas. In many ways, during those early years he was a hero to me. I went around from place to place with him, hung out in his food store, went to the flying club, he took me and my other brothers for rides in his private airplane which he owned along with other Bahamian businessmen. We were living large, as some would say today. He always bought the latest car, the best television set and we had a good supply of lunch money. Everything seemed to be going well. My family was, as you would say, your average middle to upper middle class family, and in those early days you could even say we were borderline rich.

My father owned a fairly lucrative grocery store business called Leclains Food Store. In his day and time, his stores competed head-to-head with the major food stores in Nassau. He was a well-respected businessman and well known among the elites in society. Politicians and businessmen alike would come to see him. On one occasion, I recall my father travelling to Europe along with other political dignitaries, including the country's Prime Minister. He was also a part owner of a yacht, and I can remember a few times when we went fishing with the entire family and a few friends; something the average Black family did not do in those days.

My mother stayed at home after working as a teacher for a while. The grocery business was doing quite well, so she didn't need to work. We had a maid who took care of the house cleaning and mom just took care of us in different ways. She took us to Church and cooked and spent time with us. Sometimes she was short on patience, but generally speaking, we didn't have much to worry about, because she took care of us.

I could not say that I had any intentions of being bad, selling drugs or committing acts that threatened me with punishment or jail sentences if I were caught. Sometimes I still don't understand all the reasons. One thing I learned the hard way is that life without purpose can be strange. My mom said during my early years, I gave very little indication that I would stray. As a youngster, I was quiet and well behaved. I was alone most times. She said, as a toddler, I did not say much but would act a lot louder than I spoke only if I was provoked.

I recall hearing my mom share how I would sit in a corner and mind my own business; then someone would mess with me and without a word or threat cover. I would leave my position in the corner, pop them and then return to my position. I guess I was kind of a quiet, but deadly person. Another time my mother indicated that, as an infant, I disliked the attention my baby brother was getting, so without announcement I went to the closet, picked up a bundle of shoes and proceeded to drop them on my little brother and remarked, "I knock a baby!" For some reason I didn't talk a lot to others, and that was something that carried over into my later years in high school and beyond.

As I indicated earlier, my father was not a bad person; he was a picture of the average good father in his early years. He sometimes travelled to Miami and brought gifts for the whole family. We would all gather in his bedroom to see what goodies had come from Miami for us. At that time we were like one big (with seven children) happy family.

Sometimes on Saturdays we would have family devotions and on other days we would get together, usually under my mother's guidance and sing gospel songs and read the Bible together. It is said that "The family that prays together stays together" and for a time, it seemed like that was the way it would be. I don't recall my father being there very often for devotions, but I do know that he sometimes went to Church with us. Many times he didn't go and would sit on the wall in the back of the yard drinking a few beers and entertaining his friends.

My mother said I liked Church and always sat on the front row. As early as I can recall in my own memory from a very early age, I sat on the front pew and listened to the preacher. I did not say much, but I sat and listened. As time went on, I would win prizes for good behaviour in Sunday school. I also won prizes for knowing the Bible stories, and prizes for all kinds of accomplishments in Sunday school. I liked going to Church as a youngster and I was very attentive. I sometimes wonder why I had not made a personal commitment to the Lord earlier in my life. I had fun with the Bible stories; the little games and songs in Church, but I don't remember whether I was ever introduced to the Gospel in a direct way. There were many times when inferences were made and many calls went out. As for a one-on-one conversation, I don't recall.

I remember some of the Sunday school leaders and one of the guys who led a Church group that was similar to the Boy Scouts called the Royal Rangers. Brother Ken or Ron (don't quite remember his name) was a nice guy during those early years and the other guys and I followed him. He was a nice Caucasian man from the USA, who worked with us teaching the Bible and doing activities similar to those done with the Boy Scouts. That was all very nice. As time went on, however I decided he was too soft; nothing like the guys on the streets. He did his best but to me his world was not tough or exciting for me.

One of the problems in the Church is that many male leaders are often too effeminate and not strong enough as role models for young men. Ken was one of those guys. He was a genuinely good guy but for some of us, we thought of him as a 'goofy' guy or a nerd. Don't get me wrong, he was a good guy and meant well, but he was out of touch with the real world.

Although we did a lot of nice things, I don't believe I was ever directly confronted with the Gospel on an individual basis or asked to make a decision about serving the Lord. So I enjoyed the Sunday school, the outings with Brother Ken, hanging out with the Church guys until I reached the age of about ten or eleven.

Although I had been in and out of doing bad things, I basically was still a very well behaved child; but the older I became, the more things began to change. I moved from sitting on the front pew to the middle pew and on to the back pew in Church.

The times and activities together with my father had lessened and I began to spend more and more time with my friends, who were living a different kind of life. I was gradually drifting away into another world, but neither of my parents noticed any real changes.

One of the last good memories I can recall with my father was being able to participate in the Flying contests, where his Flying Club would have a yearly competition, which required pilots to fly planes and drop bombs on targets. The bombs were actually bags of flour. They also had to fly after that and burst balloons with the propeller of the plane. I felt like a king being able to be the one to throw the 'bomb' out of the plane or just being in the crew. At that age, all I wanted to do was be a pilot when I grew up. It was a thrill to sit in the co-pilot seat and help steer the plane, as we flew around the island. I also learned a little about shooting pool at the Flying Club. These were the last 'good ole days'. As you will see times were changing.

LESSON # 1
IT'S NOT WHERE YOU ARE BORN, BUT WHAT'S BORN IN YOU

- There are people born everyday in the same place with different outcomes. It is more important what's born in you than where you are born.

- I was not born in the Ghetto but the Ghetto was born in me so I left my comfortable life to pursue something negative that was born in me.

- There are many stories we see everyday of two brothers or sisters sometimes even twins who were born in the same place, one may end up in College and the other in prison.

- Sometimes we see the Ghetto as a physical address but the reality is there are people who live in mental ghettos and spiritual ghettos which are just as disabling as physical ghettos.

- Whether you are Rich or Poor, whether you have money or fame–it does not insulate you from a poor mental state or bad choices. Rich people end up on drugs, addicted to alcohol and in prison just as poor people do. The news presents us everyday with the poor choices of people with money and fame, from DUI to various criminal activities. Money and fame are no guarantee for success or fulfillment in life.

- You don't need things to enjoy life, you need life to enjoy things!

CHAPTER 2

'VALLEY OF DECISION'

During most of my youth, I had no question about the validity or truth about the Church and God. I did not understand everything, but I believed all that stuff was real. As time moved on and I acquired new friends and was exposed to new things in the world, for the first time I began to question these things. I don't think I ever questioned in my mind whether there was a God or whether He was real, but I did begin to question the Church or at least the one I attended.

Church seemed uninteresting and boring in comparison to what was happening on the street and in the outside world. So many things seemed unexciting compared to other things I was experiencing. The parties at Church and my school friends were quite different. My friends' parties were much more exciting. So I entered what I call the 'Valley of Decision.' It was a stage where I started comparing and assessing things that I saw.

I also started questioning other things such as 'authority' and during my later years in elementary school I started taking chances and straying away from the Christian upbringing that had characterized my life up to that point. I began disobeying teachers, fighting, and thinking more about girls. I can remember on one occasion I threw a classmate down and busted his head open on a piece of metal; blood spilled all over the place. It was the first time I had done something like that and it was a scary site. I was fortunate that I did not get expelled from school. I was afraid and apologized to his parents, as he was a friend but my behaviour did not end there.

Then I started fighting with other students on and off and was generally making a nuisance of myself although it wasn't very noticeable because I was still generally well behaved. I was still doing very well in school but changes were taking place that few noticed. One of the reasons I presume was because I was always a quiet person.

Another part of my Valley of Decision related to girls. I used to hang with two other guys and we all were considered handsome or good looking. We started to talk about girls and eventually we started talking about who liked whom and what we were going to do. It was like a contest to see who had the right stuff to attract the girls. M.K, Mikey, and Davy B held court during lunch breaks with a crew of girls, talking about sex and about things young guys and girls talk about. Of course at this time none of us were sexually active, but we talked and fantasized about all of the stuff that adults were doing.

We were like the star attractions of the girls in our elementary school. We also began to do little subtle things like 'feeling' girls or kissing them on their lips or cheeks. This was an area that I had not thought about much previously, but as time went on, I began to change my view about girls and became attracted to them in a way that I had not before. My friends, Mickey D, MK and I got all the attention and recognition among the ladies as the top prizes in the school.

At the same time, I also became exposed to one or two gangsters; the kind who came to school although they were school dropouts, and robbed students of their lunch money. One of the strange things about life was that I always seemed to be attracted to these guys and they often befriended me. One such guy was named Blue, who was notorious. He would fight, rob, steal or do whatever he decided to do and was a general nuisance to the community and school. Blue later became a drug dealer, murderer and convict. For one reason or the other, he came to talk to me and we became friends. He would not rob me or take my lunch money, but from time to time he actually gave me stuff I guess as if to say, "You cool with me." We never had much contact, but a seed was planted. I had made friends with a gangster.

During that time, I was still going to Church every Sunday. I had become less interested in what was happening at Church and more and more interested in what was happening outside the Church. I secretly admired the boys on the street. My brother, who was five years older, was hanging out with these boys "on the blocks." We lived down the hill from Warren Street, where the bad boys hung out. The corner that I lived on was very quiet and everyone was generally well behaved. My early friends were cool; we would shoot marbles, play ball and ride bicycles together, all the normal things that were done by little boys.

Warren Street was a different world. The guys used to cuss and party, drink, smoke weed, and have a good time. Whatever I was into seemed so much less exciting than what was happening on Warren Street. In my mind, I just watched and took in what was happening. I watched my brother as he hung out with the boys on the block or "boys in the Hood." They seemed to be having a good time. They used to play basketball and baseball and party a lot. They also drank alcohol and hung out; it seemed like a world of fun. The name of the team many of them played was called 'Warriors.' I often went to the games that were held in an old gym and cheer for my brother's team. After the games they would drink, get drunk, talk foolishness and have what seemed to be a good time.

After watching my brother and his friends, one day I decided that it was time for me to start cussing. Neither my mother or father used to cuss openly, but my life was changing and I was evaluating life and drawing my own conclusions. I was the only one who really knew what was going on with me. My mother thought I was still the best boy around and in some ways I was. But mothers always see the good in their children and have a hard time seeing the bad.

After evaluating the situation in my mind as I often did, I decided that I was missing something. As a result of this decision, I went around the corner and climbed an almond tree and sat there for several hours and cussed my head off. I started cussing, "mother……sh….,da….gd….." every word that I could think of I used. I cussed and cussed and cussed, I guess it was so I could get it out of my system and practice for the future.

During that time as was custom, every year my mother used to take most of the family to Miami. We would check into a hotel in downtown Miami and go shopping and sightseeing. It was wonderful. We always had a good time. Often my cousins would travel with us at the same time and we would all go out together.

As time went on and I had begun to change further, I went from cussing to stealing and being a general nuisance in a variety of ways. We would go to Miami and my younger brother, who was always considered to be the mischievous one of the family, along with my cousin 'Dickey' and I would wreak havoc wherever we went. Our parents still didn't know what was happening. We would go to the top of the hotel roof and spit on people who were walking below. Other times we would throw water on people who walked below. Then when we were finished, we would start at the top floor and go straight to the bottom floor and kick and bang on every door, then run out of the fire escape and laugh until we were tired.

People would come out of their rooms in their robes and cuss at us. They would call the hotel security, but we never got caught. On one occasion, the hotel Security asked us whether we had seen some young men causing trouble and we said "Yes, 'they went that way.' You see, we didn't look like we would cause any trouble. We all looked innocent and were guests of the hotel, so they didn't think it was us.

As if that was not enough, we would go into department stores and go up the wrong way on escalators, slide down the middle, run all around the store and create all kinds of havoc. We were always careful to not let our parents know what was happening. We then graduated from simple horseplay to stealing, shoplifting or 'teefing' as Bahamians would say.

Our neighbours, Carlton and Keith, used to play with my brother and me. They introduced us to Hot Wheel cars and we used to set up tracks and race one another. Carlton and Keith would always beat us, because they had the latest model cars. We were desperately trying to catch up, so we had a plan. We decided that while in Miami we would stock up on Hot Wheel cars that were not yet available in Nassau. The only thing was we didn't have enough money to buy all we wanted. So my brother and I went into a large department store and after checking for Security, we took a shopping bag and walked down the aisle and one of us swooped a whole section of Hot Wheel cars into the bag while the other held the bag open. When we returned to Nassau, we won all the races. As time went on, this continued every year and we would steal new items, shoes, clothes, toys, anything that we could get away with.

As I was coming to the end of my elementary school career and had begun to cause trouble at school, I found myself being sent to the Principal's Office to be punished with a cane whipping by Reverend Saunders, the school principal. He was a famous Bahamian educator who wielded a serious cane and made many a young tough guy beg for mercy. I took my licks, but I also began to learn the tricks of the trade. Instead of going to the Principal's Office when the teacher sent me for disciplinary action, I would go to the bathroom, beat my hands on the wall, wet my face and rub my eyes so I could look like I had been crying from my whipping. I remained out for a while before slowly entering the class. It worked well and I had learned how to beat the system.

I still had to go to Church each week, because my mother insisted and my father did too, although he often did not go himself. This bothered me, but I did not say much. I became less and less attracted to Church as it became less relevant to me. Church seemed to be a nice place, but something was missing. It was like nothing was happening there.

I also became afraid of Church. Many times the pastor or preacher would say.... "You could die tomorrow and your soul will end up in hell".... I did not want to go to hell, but neither could I see myself becoming a Christian. Christianity seemed to be too soft, too feminine, and too out of touch with the real world. So I moved from the front row in the Church to the back row, often sleeping through the entire Service only to be disturbed by the "Altar call."

As time went by, I dreaded going to Church to the point where I didn't look forward to Sunday mornings. I used to go there and remain in the car and sleep or go inside for the beginning of the Service and then leave shortly after. I felt a little ashamed that I still had to go to Church because most of my friends did not have to go. In fact, sometimes on my way to Church we would pass the corner where I hung out, and to make sure that my friends didn't see me going to Church, I would lie down in the car. I had decided I was into a different life and Church was a liability.

As my mind began to toggle between the Church and the 'real world,' I received a dose of some things that would shape my world as time went on. I used to love comic books and bought a lot. One day a friend and I noticed that one of the local news companies was located near my house and they often left many of the comic books in their vans on the weekend. We discussed our plan and decided to raid the vans and steal the 'funny' books as we called them. One Saturday night, we climbed the fence and proceeded to enter the vans stacked with comic books and we stole loads and loads of them. We tried not to take too many because the owners might miss them, and we would not have our supply.

We did this for a couple months before the owners realized someone was breaking into the vans and stealing their comic books. Often when I went to school I was the king there, because I had all the latest: Spiderman, Superman, Captain America and the Fantastic Four comics. I had suitcases full of comic books: Batman, Wonder Woman, and just about every other comic book you could think of. I used to sell them at times, but I would mostly give them to my friends while keeping my own collection.

It was at that time, too, that I was introduced or introduced myself to some other books that would change my life and my innocence. The news company I stole from also carried Playboy, Penthouse and Hustler magazines. I often broke into one of the vans as usual and stole what I thought were comic books, but it was not until I got home that I realized these "comic" books were very different. I stared at the pictures of naked women and sex scenes that permanently altered my young mind.

Although those books were not my primary interest at that time, I stole them which meant that my young mind was being influenced and permanently damaged by something that would later become an addiction and a negative factor in my life – pornography.

Those first instances of stealing in Miami and stealing comic books would form habits later in life that would be hard to break and would eventually get me into trouble.

After these early experiences my next adventure was breaking into cars. I used to hang out with a guy, whose nickname was 'Al Capone' and he was my cousin. Al was in trouble from the time he could walk. If you didn't know what to do in terms of something wrong, Al Capone knew it and did it. I can recall an incident where he and my younger brother and I were stealing "reflector lights" off bicycles. Everyone knew Capone was headed for trouble.

During that time my father instituted a curfew for my brother and me. We had to be home by 9:00 p.m. most of the time. I would make sure that I made it home in time, but my younger brother would always come home late and get a whipping. Almost every night he would get the same punishment, as he continually came home too late.

One of the things Capone did was break into cars at a local car dealership and just drive them around the car lot. At one point in time he and other friends banged up a number of the cars and had to go to court but were not sentenced. I took a cue from Capone and as proximity was again in my favour, there was a car dealership near my house, so sometimes alone and sometimes with a friend I would go into the lot and break into the cars, take out cassette players, radios and tapes or other items that were left in them and keep them for myself or sell them.

One day a neighbour saw me jumping the fence near the lot and she began to scold me and ask what I had done and I proceeded to cuss her out. She told my parents, but I explained that I didn't say what she thought I said. Some of our neighbours began to notice something different about me as I cursed the same lady out again on another occasion. I also beat up some of the boys in the neighbourhood. One time I beat my neighbour with a stick, so everyone began to notice that I was a little different than they knew me to be. Fortunately for me, I was still well behaved at home so my mother especially took note of what was said about me, but it was hard for her to believe the negative reports, because I had never caused a problem at home. I was still very quiet and co-operative.

During that same time, I also began to experience my first 'real' parties. Previously I had only been to Church parties, my Church friends' parties, and parties in my neighbourhood. Church parties were totally boring to me. Often it seemed like there was a 'Nerd' disease running around when comparing the Church group to friends I had in the everyday world.

My parents were very strict when I was young. They did not let us go to the movies and we couldn't go to certain types of parties, so much of what I was accustomed to took place at Church. Suddenly I was involved in all the things my parents kept from me. I started going to the movies and watching movies that were not designed for minors. I also took my first drink of alcohol at a party held at a friend's house. I slow danced for the first time and the list goes on and on. The main thing about this period was that once again my world was changing. I had reached the unfortunate conclusion that life was better on the wild side.

Although my father and I communicated when I was very young, as time went on, we had less communications. He was busy with his grocery business and he became less loyal to his household, something most of the children would not know about or understand right away. He seemed to be such a good father at the time. While this was happening, I was forming my own world views and my father's world and mine were totally different. Neither he nor my mother knew just how much my world was changing, but it certainly was.

In the final analysis I weighed the odds and decided that I wanted to be like my older brother and his friends. I actually longed for the day to come when I could hang out on the corner, smoke weed and drink like my brother. That seemed to be the best or most attractive option at the time.

LESSON #2
ASSOCIATIONS AFFECT DESTINATION

- Bad company corrupts–This scripture quote explains the effect of negative associations "Do not be misled: Bad company corrupts good character."

- Who you hang around is who you become. If you are a part of a group of four friends and three have already gone to prison, you are next if you remain a part of that group.

- You will be like your associations. If you want to see what your future looks like check where your friends are headed. If they are going in a positive direction, you are likely to be headed there, if they are going in a negative direction, you are likely to be headed there also.

- Associations multiply what's in you. If you like to do wrong and you hook up with similar people it's very likely that your journey into wrong will be accelerated because your friends tend to enhance and accelerate your behavior, negative or positive

- People should qualify to be in your life. Your friends should have to pass a test to be with you. That test should be based upon whether they improve your life or make it worse. Real friends improve your life and make your situation better.

CHAPTER 3

'EVANGELIZED BY THE GANGSTERS'

As a young teen, I was already becoming a menace in many ways, but life changed significantly for me in the months that followed my entry into Jr. High School. The first major incident was when a teacher tried to confiscate my radio.

There was a rule in the school that you could not have personal electronics on campus, but as usual, I defied the rule. So she came to me and asked me to turn it in. I said I was not turning it in and asked her to leave me alone. She said I could get suspended from school and that I had to give it up. I told her I paid my money for it so I was not giving it to her. Then she came up to me and tried to take it. I was infuriated and proceeded to throw her on the ground when she reached for it.

The other students could not believe what happened and they knew I would be suspended or expelled. The teacher called the vice principal and he came and took me to his office, where I received a lecture and was suspended from school for two weeks. I returned to school after the suspension and ended up in another critical situation that changed my life.

One Tuesday afternoon around 3:30 p.m. at the young age of twelve, a few friends and I were in a classroom at my High School, Government High, when a rough and tough young man entered the door way and quickly proclaimed, "Everyone out the xxxxxxx room." Everyone knew who he was and quickly obeyed his command. This was TW, who was famous for robbing students and everything else imaginable. TW had already dropped out of school a long time and would come to our school to rob and beat up students.

One time TW lined a group of my friends up on a straight line and told them to stand at attention. While they were standing at attention, he quickly went into their pockets and relieved them of all of their cash or valuables. After taking their money he pulled out a knife, cut up their pants and told them to go home. That day when he entered the classroom I didn't move. He motioned as if to say "What's wrong with you boy, don't you know who I am?" As he came towards me, I stood there and did not crack a smile or move. I thought he was going to punch me or whack me with something, but he suddenly stopped and almost fell on the ground laughing. He looked at me and said, "I like you, you are a crazy lil red nigger."

Then he invited me to come with him back to his hood, an area called Bain Town or 'the Bottom.' He took me into this ghetto area and we started hanging out together. I felt proud that I could be in the company of TW. I don't know why but he just clicked with me so we started hanging out, smoking weed and getting in trouble. TW was so bad he didn't live in his parents' house. He had his own little house in their back yard made of wood, like a chicken coop. At first, I was a little afraid to smoke marijuana, but he assured me that all the talk about flying off buildings and going crazy was just foolishness and was a way to make you afraid of something that was 'nice.' He called it 'the weed of wisdom.'

Our friendship soon escalated and we started to hang together a lot. Many days he would meet me at the end of the school's fence, where we would smoke some weed and talk. Sometimes we would go into a food store nearby and TW would say, "This is my dad's food store, just take what you want, everything is cool." Knowing the reputation of TW, I would just go into the food store and take stuff off the shelf, put it in my bag and walk out. If the Security or employees said anything, TW would slap them or issue threats and everything would be cool.

This continued until one day I was helping myself and got caught by the Security. As I was about to be escorted to the manager's office, TW came and told Security to let me go. They began to argue and the Security ran in the office knowing TW's reputation. He locked the door and they were exchanging words back and forth with TW not knowing that Security had pushed the panic button and the police had already been called.

As they were continuing their conversation, I was let go and I saw the police before TW did, so I shouted to him and took off. He narrowly got away from the police and we ran and ran until we came to a Church nearby where another of my gangster friends lived. He was called GF.

I used to think TW was crazy and he was definitely kind of crazy. Sometimes he would pick me up on his motorcycle and we would be riding down the road and he would close his eyes while riding the bike and laugh and ask me if his eyes were closed or not. Sometimes we almost got into accidents or almost got killed. I was losing a lot of fears and was taking my own chances.

In addition to smoking weed, TW would give me some pills from time to time. He gave me all kinds of drugs. I don't even remember what some of them were but I remember the names Orange Sunshine, Purple Haze (LSD), Hashish, Speed, Paper Acid and others that I can't recall at the moment. I took some, sold some and gave some to others.

TW was always in fights and the fact that he was my friend gave me a certain status in school. He used to beat up students all the time. Only one time I remember a student fighting back. This student I remember as BJ who cut TW in his face with a barber razor and left some gaping scars on his face. After this BJ couldn't come to school or had to constantly hide. TW finally caught up with him, took his track shoes and beat him in his head and face with the spiked shoes until bystanders pleaded for him to stop as the School Security arrived. I thought TW was going to kill BJ, but fortunately intervention came at the right time.

Another friend I started to hang out with was my cousin GF, who was like TW in a lot of ways. In addition, GF was into other things like Junkanoo. Junkanoo is a local festival in some ways like a carnival or madigras. It was a rite of passage in the Bahamas for a young man to be involved with Junkanoo, so when GF introduced me to the powers that be, I became interested in Junkanoo and joined the group known as the Vikings. The main territory where the Vikings hung out was called "Harlem," nicknamed after Harlem, New York, because it was an area notorious for fighting and trading everything from marijuana, to cocaine and weapons.

GF and I hung together and did petty crimes like shoplifting. We smoked weed together and he let me know that if I needed protection it would be no problem. We also went into the same food store that I went into with TW and we also did the same things. He had the same type of reputation as TW and he also spent time stealing and intimidating Security and store employees.

I can recall some occasions where we stole almost shelves full of stuff. One day I packed about fifteen of the little mini drinks in my bag and a variety of snacks. I thought it was funny. GF was from an area called Farrington Road. Some days after school, we would hang together with another notorious youth in that area called JQ. As time passed, I was introduced to more members of the gangster's league.

Another friend I picked up along the way was KT, who was a nice guy but one of his brothers had a reputation for being one of the worst dudes in the Bahamas; he was feared all over Nassau. KT was from Harlem. As I noted earlier, Harlem was a tough place. It was not often that you would mess with someone from Harlem and get away with it. You were in the big time if you had the brothers from Harlem on your side.

KT also was a student at the High School I attended. He was a pretty quiet person, but also deadly. We met at Government High. One afternoon I was in the boys' locker room and two guys who were known for being bad boys in the school were in the process of beating all students who came into locker room if they didn't give up on their money or sometimes just because they felt like it. These two guys were friends of KT and they approached me to do a number on me.

By this time I was not the nice little boy who entered the school and I was not about to let anyone beat me, so I quickly let them know that I would xxxxx them up personally if they messed with me. They laughed and proceeded to corner me. As they did KT said, "Hold up man, I know this dude." He then turned to them and said this is Chimmy B's brother.

I was ready to go down fighting but my brother was a gangster himself and he used to hang out in Harlem so they got the hint that it was not a good idea to mess with me. They left me alone and we all became friends once they realized who I was and who my boys were.

KT and I talked and smoked weed together during lunch breaks and we became good friends. I remember him talking to me about fighting. He was not a real big guy, but he told me how to beat up the big guys.

I was tall for my age but I was slim, so he proceeded to give me some lessons on how to deal with people no matter what their size. He noted that you have to take them off their legs, strike first and jump all over them and take their nerve. I never forgot that lesson. I often stopped by KT's place in Harlem, and it was there that I met others from Harlem and learned new tricks of the street trade.

In Harlem I learned how to shoot dice, play cards and dominoes for money and smoke hashish. I met and became friends with the top gangsters and they let me know that if I needed them to take care of anyone (meaning beat up), just let them know. These guys were hard core; many were wanted by the police and were constantly in trouble. They had legendary nicknames like Shaft, Poker, Boom Clark, Nugget, Kali and others. I used to hang with all of them and when people saw me with them they realized that I had moved into a different league.

Sometimes I left school early so I could hang with the boys from Harlem. Often we would shoot pool at a restaurant and bar in the area called The Shoal. Other times, we would just chill on the street corner and smoke some weed. To be able to hang out in Harlem and to have the guys in Harlem as your friends was a tremendous asset at that time in the underworld. It was an asset on the street level, but a liability if you were trying to behave.

Harlem was feared and respected all over Nassau. In fact, in my school I was even more feared than before when other guys in the school would see me with the gangsters from Harlem.

I remember the feeling I had when guys from Harlem would come to the school to bring me stuff and talk with me. Nugget, Shaft, DT and others would come by the school to watch games or just hang out. They would always bring weed to smoke and would fool around with the girls.

Two of the worst areas in Nassau at that time were Harlem and Bain Town aka "The Bottom" and I had friends in both areas. There was one time when I ended up in the middle of a clash between Harlem and The Bottom. TW and I were talking on the school ground when DT from Harlem came up to us and he wasn't smiling. Of course I was cool with him, but he had a problem with TW. Before I could blink my eyes, DT had punched TW, thrown him on the ground and started stomping on him. TW got up and ran to bring back about ten guys from The Bottom. Within that short period of time, DT had also rounded up his crew from Harlem. It seemed like they were about to go at it when one of the guys from Harlem started to talk to one of the guys from the Bottom. The neighbourhoods were fairly close to each other and sometimes they did drug transactions together, so they had a last minute talk and in the end they just walked away from each other.

During this time while I was hanging out in Harlem and the Bottom, I was also hanging out in the main area where I grew up. Actually this area was home base even though I spent a lot of time in Harlem and The Bottom. We called it The University of Warren Street. My brother used to hang out in Harlem a lot but his home base was also Warren Street.

Whatever I didn't learn from TW and the guys in Harlem, I learned from my friends at The University of Warren Street. Cheese, Knox, Bobo and 007 were my early mentors on Warren Street. I was actually the youngest on my block, but I was taller than most other guys my age. CH and 007 and I started out smoking cigarettes, then I graduated to weed and along with KX and BB, and I got my introduction to the party life, sexy girls and night clubbing.

The strangest thing about this was my age of 15 years old when I started going to nightclubs. Sometimes the nightclub owners would not let my friends in who were older than me and I would still get in. A whole group of us used to go to a nightclub in the area called the Banana Boat and dance and drink and chill. Often we would smoke weed before we got to the club. After coming from the nightclub we would sit on the corner late at night and laugh and talk, gamble and tell jokes until 2 or 3 a.m. Anyone who could get access to a car was the one who would be the hero when we were going out. Eventually i would use my little brother to sneak into my mothers bedroom, steal her keys, then i would take the keys and steal her car, go out all night and then push the car back into the garage and jump through the window. I stole my mothers car many times and she had no idea because after clubbing i would always put the keys back in her purse and the car would be where she left it.

CH's father was a former police inspector, who had a severe drinking problem. He would always be outside the house late at night telling jokes and yelling the top of his voice "Yippee! - Drunk again!" We would all laugh as he told dirty jokes. He used to get angry at us for smoking weed in his yard and often threatened to call the police. It really used to be fun hanging out on the corner until late in the morning. All of us used to sit on the wall and imitate CH's dad saying "Yippee" and "My Brother" and "Drunk Again" among other things.

I started to do a lot of crazy stuff in school. I would slap other students, rob them, and make them pay me to go inside the lunch room. I started doing so many things that I was constantly having to go to the principal's office.

One time they brought several school administrators to get me. I had cursed out a teacher so they came to reprimand me. I acted like I didn't know what they were talking about, but I went with them and they gave me a tongue lashing and wanted to know if I was taking drugs. I didn't reply. They thought something was wrong with me, so they tried to get me to see a psychiatrist. I said "no way."

I was suspended from school again and my parents were called in. After serving my suspension I was able to come back to school after my mother had spoken with the principal and they agreed to give me another chance. None of this really bothered me much, because I was living in another world.

It was during this time that communication with my parents was very minimal. Little was asked of me and I volunteered little. They did ask who my new friends were but I always had an excuse. My dad was very busy with his business, so we never did talk much, except when there was a report from the school that I had done something out of the way. Although my mother and I talked, I only let her know what I wanted to let her know. When I got kicked out of school I would explain to her how it was the teachers' fault and how they didn't understand Bahamians, since many of the teachers were from England.

I loved my mother and she always tried to get me to go to Church. She would pray for me and my other brothers and always believed the best about me. When I was around her, I was always quiet and did not make much of a fuss. In a way, I admired her and her strong Christian stand, but I just could not see myself into that at the time because it seemed like Church was not cool. At times, I would go to Church with her, but I always sat in the back of the Church and slept. So many times I would be out partying and in the nightclubs and would often come home late on a Sunday morning and would still be high by the time I went to Church.

I guess I lived in two different worlds. One world was of a generally nice boy at home, except for a few occasions when I would do things; sometimes because I was high. The other world was school drug dealer and young street disciple.

My mother really tried to teach me the right way and my father tried to some extent, but primarily my mother did her best to teach me about God and make sure that I went to Church and lived right. While my parents were teaching me one thing, my friends at the Junkanoo Shack, Warren Street and Harlem were teaching me another.

There were all types of guys at the Junkanoo Shack; businessmen, respectable citizens, drug dealers, criminals of all assortments and I learned from them and made my contributions of teaching others along the way. The lessons of Harlem and Warren Street seemed so much more appealing than what my parents or other adults had to say. I figured they didn't know and couldn't understand my world. On the corner or hanging with the boys in the neighbourhood, everything was cool; there was always a party, always a free high and always acceptance.

There was a sense of security and belonging being around the guys. It was a kind of freedom. No one was asking where you've been or what you have or haven't done. Everything was just cool. Of course everybody had a nickname. Your nickname was like your calling card. It was a positive stroke for your ego. At first they called me Dave the Butcher in school. My second nickname was Miguel as my middle name was Michael and that was a Spanish pronunciation. Later my nickname changed to Davy B since they used to call my brother Chimmy B. Finally one of the guys, Rasta' from my neighbourhood, nicknamed me 'Pork-man', a terminology used among Rastas for light skinned blacks.

By this time, in my life I was no longer on the fence trying to determine my course in life. I was full fledged on the other side. The street was my real home. I just went home for the necessities. I did not identify with my parents or my family in terms of fellowship or friendship. All my friends hung out in the same place. I was now a full-fledged convert. It was time to start Living Large as some would say!

LESSON #3
DISCOVERING YOUR DESTINY

- One of the greatest discoveries of life is where you are not supposed to be. I learned through time and experiences that I was in the wrong place. I could not see it at first because I was blinded but I was not supposed where I was headed.

- We are all "Destined for Glory" by God, he planned a good life for each of us, if you are not in or headed in a "Glorious" direction then it means that you have ignored your true destiny and you are living below where you should be.

- If you don't know your destination you could end up in the wrong place. The Prodigal Son came from an affluent caring family but ended up feeding pigs and living in a place that was not his natural destiny.

- When you recognize you are in the wrong place, it is time to "come to your senses" and head back in the direction of your destiny.

- In the story of the prodigal he realized he did not belong with swine, it was not his destiny.

- Prison is not the destiny that God planned for anyone, prison is the wrong place. Being unmarried and having children and living in poverty is not your destiny.

- I eventually discovered that Prison was not where I was supposed to be, I was not supposed to be selling drugs or using drugs, I discovered my destiny and changed course. It is never too late to change course but it's important to change early in life, the longer you wait the harder it gets.

CHAPTER 4

'LIVIN LARGE'

One afternoon on Warren Street, I received a lesson that was a kind of 'rite of passage.' Up to this time I had not been arrested although I had some close calls. This time I was in real danger of being arrested by the Police. We were all sitting on the corner when the Police came by and indicated to us that we would have to move. There was an unwritten law against groups of young men assembled in public areas. They were attempting to break up these groups and gangs and limit their influence. So they told us to move. Nobody moved. One of the officers told the other to get the handcuffs. DC told the officer that if he went for the handcuffs they would be wrapped around his neck. Rudolpho told the officer that he would stomp on his chest if he tried anything. Sensing that the two of them would not get very far with us they left, or so we thought. As they left they simply reversed down the street to call for backups. We decided to move on before they came back with reinforcements.

Around this same time, another friend named Black and I decided to catch a ride with one of the ladies in the neighbourhood. As we got in the car and pulled off three police cars pulled up. One was in front of the car; one on the passenger side and one in the back. That left only one route of escape. We jumped out of the car and began to run from the two officers who were in hot pursuit. As we ran DC threw a big rock at one of the officers and narrowly missed him; this gave us time to get away. As we sprinted away into a neighbour's yard, more police officers came from another direction. This time they had us cornered. They grabbed Black but as they grabbed his shirt he wiggled and left the officer with a shirt in his hands. This gave me time to run. I ran and ran until I got away and met up with some of the other guys who had escaped. Police were all over the neighbourhood. I breathed a sigh of relief and waited until the heat was off then walked through the bushes home.

By the time I reached age 14, I was official. I was ruler of my territory at school and I hung with the meanest dudes in the business. The things and people I was around were among the most notorious in Nassau. I saw things at a young age that many older persons had not seen.

I hung around drug dealers, bank robbers, rapists, murderers, con men and every other type person you could imagine. I was just a youngster, but I felt very comfortable with these guys. Most of them looked out for me and took me in like a son. Some didn't know me at first but they never troubled me because I was a part of the crew. I was there as they cleaned their guns in the shack. I was there when the drug shipments came in and we would be "baggin up" (placing the drugs in plastic bags for sale).

I remember one time when one of the guys we used to call "Claw" had stolen a police cache of guns and everyone in our area had a variety of guns. I really wanted a gun at that time, but was told I was too young and they did not want me to do anything stupid with it, so I had to wait until a few months later before getting my hands on my first gun.

After being converted to these guys, I became their evangelist; I was like those who introduced me to the world of 'street life 101.' I terrorized my school. Many days I would go to school and smoke weed while wearing my dark shades. If anyone came too close or especially if someone laughed in my vicinity, I would slam them. Some students would get slapped, kicked or punched every time I saw them.

Sometimes when I arrived at school, students would run out of the hallways and into their classrooms because they saw me coming. As time went on, I began to get worse and worse. I started having dice games in the school's bathrooms and taking the money of the guys I shot dice with. Many students were bigger than me, but very few would even consider getting into anything with me, because they thought I was a crazy. I had attempted to stab another student with a blade and had consistently assaulted fellow students for the slightest reason and sometimes for no reason at all. In any case, students knew that I could call TW, GF or my crew from Warren Street or Harlem, and they knew that my boys would back me up if necessary.

To this day, I don't really understand why but I had turned into a genuinely mean person. Some days I would remain after school and rob the school's soda machines. Sometimes I would break the machines up and when they fixed them, I would break them again. At other times, I would stand at the lunchroom door and tax students who wanted to buy lunch. I would stand at the door and let them know they would have to pay in order to enter. At other times, I took students' lunch money or took items from them that they brought to school.

On one occasion, I broke into the school's storage facilities and stole hundreds of school books, which I then re-sold to students at a discounted price. I don't know exactly why but sometimes I would get angry for no reason. On the covers of all my books I would write in big bold letters F……..You! Some days I just decided that I didn't want anyone to talk to me and if someone who I did not like came to talk to me I would punch them.

It was at this age that I started my own gang in school. I was still young and the gang was not like gangs of today, but it was one of the first "mini" gangs. A friend called Skeeter and I, after seeing a movie on gangs that was supposed to help young people stay away form gangs, formed a group called "Ben Up's". Our motto was, "We will bend your xxxx xxxxx up." The Ben Up's terrorized some of the students in the school for a short time and eventually disbanded, since there was really no one there to fight.

Shortly after we had disbanded, my friend Skeeter was constantly taking all kinds of drugs and I advised him to stop taking sleeping pills, because they made him fall all over the place and get into fights, and he would get beat up after school. After some discussion we got into a shoving match and I threw him on the ground and knocked his head into a desk. I didn't realize he had a knife at the time, but as we tussled he pulled out the knife and we fought for it. He was able to retrieve the knife and he tried to stab me, but I was able to escape. I went outside and picked up some big rocks and came back after him. I stood in front of him with the rocks in my hand and he was standing there with the knife. Other students in the school started screaming and were afraid of what would happen.

Fortunately we were able to sort things out. This was my boy and we stared at each other probably both thinking why were we doing this when we supposed to be friends. We ended up resolving the dispute and resumed being friends. Some of the students were freaking out because they thought either I would kill him or he would kill me. Thank God we both caught ourselves and ended the dispute.

By now I was finding ways to engage in all kinds of illegal activities. I remember being in Biology class in school and receiving a lesson on how to grow seeds. The teacher asked us to do an experiment at home where we would take bean seeds and place them in a jar with tissue so they would spring and we should report on what we learned. I thought to myself "bean seeds?", I have some other seeds I would like to grow so I proceeded to try the experiment with marijuana and it worked so I ended up starting my own marijuana farm on a neighbours property. The neighbour had some property with a lot of bush and overgrown trees on a hill so I planted my seeds on his property. I used to call the hill reefer mountain because me and a friend used to go up to the hill and smoke my home grown plants in the bushes.

I was also selling drugs on the school campus. My brother, who in many ways provided the inspiration for me to want to be a gangster, used to bring big grocery bags of drugs home and we along with some of his friends who were much older than me, package the drugs for sale. Sometimes he would give me a free high and there were other times when I would get packages from him to sell in school or I would take packages that I got from him and re-package them in order to make more money.

I started selling joints or half bags of weed to students in the school and other times I would take drugs to school to smoke with my friends. I remember days when I would look under my brother's mattress and find hundreds of $10.00 and $5.00 packages lined off. Some times I would steal packages from him and sell them to make extra money or smoke them with friends.

My brother, MK who was my brother's drug business partner, and I would get a big pair of scissors to cut up the marijuana. We would then separate the weed into half bags, bags or ounces. As we bagged the weed, we would sample it to insure the quality. Some of the drugs came from Jamaica; we used to call it Jamaican "Collie" and some came from Colombia that had a golden look; we used to call it "Colombian Gold", which used to give a serious high.

My brother and MK were the main drug dealers in our area, but they were connected to gangsters from all over the Bahamas. Many of the top gangsters used to see me and would give me cash because of who my brother was. My brother was never what I would consider a violent gangster, but he was wicked. He was very sociable so he got along with everyone and for some reason they trusted him. Sometimes they came by our house and hang out in the back yard, and at other times they met on the blocks or in the shack.

Two of the most famous guys were AK 47 and Dirty Red (names altered slightly). These two would kill in a minute. AK 47 and Dirty Red were famous for robbing other drug dealers, including Colombian drug dealers. It was amazing to see how they stayed alive. There were many rumors on the street about them and there were incidences where some of their friends ended up shot to death; and the word on the street was that the Colombians had retaliated.

During one particular period that was really crazy in the Bahamas, there was a National election. This election went down in history as the most violent ever in the Bahamas. There were two parties seeking election at the time and both had goon squads. The Progressive Liberal Party and the Free National Movement as they were called hired young gangsters to campaign and in some cases to rein terror on the other party. The group that hung out in Warren Street and Harlem for the most part was the FNM group, although we had some guys who worked for the PLP. My brother, being a wicked gangster, worked for both groups. He campaigned for one party and got paid; then he worked for the other party and also got paid by them.

As I mentioned earlier, the Junkanoo Shack was a place of meetings for a variety of reasons. The Shack in our area was a huge warehouse. Our area was known as Warren Street or as we renamed it the "University of Warren Street". During this election period or the time leading up to it, I witnessed one of the greatest collections of gangsters in the history of the Bahamas for one purpose. As I sat among these guys I felt proud that I was associated with the likes of Poker, Ak47, the Priest, Shaft, Claw, Willy B, Lil Poker, the Dirty Red, Goon, and the list could go on for days. These guys all drove rented cars financed by the party or party backers and they would often say that financing came from US gangsters.

These guys would meet on our blocks every now and then, mostly on Fridays; many times they would have rolls of 50 and 100 bills and would get together and smoke weed, shoot dice and talk about things to come. They also had a lot of cocaine and would get together and snort it. Sometimes they talked about things they did, other times they talked about things they were going to do. They talked about shooting up the opposition party headquarters, burning down buildings that belonged to the opposition, terrorizing opposition officials and just about anything else you could imagine.

Sometimes I would sit and listen to plans being made and a few days or the next day, I would read about the incident in the newspaper. I remember one of the guys telling us he had burned down the food store of a famous PLP supporter, and we all laughed about it. The incident was all over the news.

Another time, one of the guys talked about shooting up the headquarters of the PLP in an area called Fox Hill. One incident that stuck in my mind was the day I sat on the corner with one of the guys who worked for the FNM. His name, Barry Major, was well known in Bahamian history. He sat and played dominoes with us, we joked around and talked, and a few days later I picked up the newspaper and saw that he was dead, murdered by Lil Poker and "Red" Burrows.

Many days on Warren Street, we talked about this incident and one of the guys who was on the scene of the murder reflected on what happened and we laughed about it. We laughed as they talked about how he took off when the first shot was fired. Ironically after Lil Poker was captured, he escaped and one night as we were playing dominoes at the University, Lil Poker showed up and called out one of his friends.

After some discussion it was decided that all of us would walk together up the street so the CID (Criminal Investigative Division) and other police officers would not recognize that Lil Polka was among us. We walked for a while and DC and NP decided that Lil Poker would be staying in our Junkanoo Shack, because it would be a difficult place for the police to find. The junkanoo Shack was a big warehouse in the bushes and only a little track road gave any indication as to its entrance. After Lil Polker was safe, I started to walk to the track road that led to the Shack. As I was about to enter the track road, the police pulled up alongside me and one of the officers who knew me asked, "Davy B, where Poker is man, I know you'll have him round here", I laughed and said I did not see him and did not know where he was.

I kept walking because I was right near the entrance of the track road and if I stayed in that area they might notice. They kept driving next to me and I kept telling them I heard he had escaped from jail but had no idea where he was. They drove off after not getting any information from me and I breathed a sigh of relief. They kept circling the area, but no one would provide them with information so they left.

If they had pressed or even if they had noticed the track road they may have gotten him. Of course on the street none of us would ever give the police information. Poker stayed in the Shack for few days and NP and DC took food to him. After a few days he was transferred to an old abandoned building in an area known as Prospect Ridge, where he set up camp along with another friend who used to rob banks. NP and DC would take them food, clothes and would sometimes take girlfriends to him. After being at the abandoned building for a while they moved to a vacant house in an area called the White Grove.

After hiding out successfully for a while, one day DC went to take some items to Poker only to meet the house surrounded by police officers from the CID. As gunfire started to flare up there, DC sped off and after an exchange of fire, which a police officer was shot; Poker was captured and eventually executed for murder.

To many I guess some of these things may have been scary, but I was proud to go to school and tell my friends, whom I hung out with and what kind of action I was around and involved in. The stories I had for school friends were mind boggling.

One night just before the election, my friends Knox and Mikey, who was older than us, decided to go to the headquarters of the FNM on Poinciana Drive as some action was about to go down. When we arrived at the headquarters all three of us went into the yard and watched, as some of our friends and the guys I mentioned earlier were loading guns, machetes and other weapons into their cars. Big B came out of the building and announced,

"The man don't want to see no PLP cars on the road". Of course Knox and I wanted to go on this mission, but we were told to go home because this was going to be some serious business and we were too young. Mickey went on the "mission" but we didn't go back home, we stayed around the area not wanting to go back to Warren Street and miss the action. As we stayed around the area, a truck came by with a group of opposition supporters and they were promptly pelted with rocks and bottles, and they sped off screaming from the attack.

We stayed around for a while longer in the area called Black Village and waited to see what else would be happening that night. As I sat on the wall along with others, the truck that was there earlier, returned but this time I heard what I thought was fire crackers, and then I heard more fire crackers. Then I saw the fire from those firecrackers and saw everybody diving for cover. It was then that I realized that bullets were being fired in my direction, so I jumped over the wall and stayed on the ground until the truck passed and the gunfire ceased.

At the same time that the truck was passing, a number of the guys I mentioned earlier were in a house in Black Village and they returned the fire at the truck that passed. Later I learned that five to seven people had received gunshot wounds. It was then that I realized I just missed getting shot myself. I actually saw the fire from the gun and heard as the bullets hit the wall, but thankfully I did not get hit. I had another story to talk about when the boys got together to smoke weed at school.

As time passed, I progressed in what I call my Living Large stage. When I went to school, I represented Warren Street and Harlem and felt it necessary for everyone to know who 'Davy B' was so I terrorized my school. At one point I ended up getting barred from the lunchroom for a year after getting caught stealing items. I used to steal entire boxes of lunch that belonged to classes and my friends and I would eat lunch and smoke weed in an abandoned building in the bushes.

I also played on the school basketball team and was an occasional starter. As time went on, however, my mind got more and more wicked. At basketball games, sometimes I would break up the games along with another friend called Dice. On one occasion we did not like the way the Referee was calling the game, so he and I threw chairs on the court. When the Referee complained, we threatened him. On one occasion he was afraid to leave the gym and had to be escorted out by bodyguards.

Sometimes when teams visited, my friend Skeeter and I would break into the locker room through a special entry we knew of and proceed to steal money, watches, jewelry and other items from the visiting team and our own team. After stealing these items we would then go to the liquor store and buy wine and liquor, and off to the drug pusher across the street in the "Bottom" and then go to the food store and buy food and pastries and have our own private party on the school grounds with a few friends playing dominoes and cards, cussing and laughing away.

Another thing that I used to do was put drugs into girls' drinks at school. We would drop pills into different girls' drinks and sit in the back of the classroom and wait until they got high and just laugh and laugh. At times I would use this tactic to take advantage of girls. Sometimes the girls would really freak out and have to be taken to the Office because they would do all kinds of strange things. Eventually one girl figured out what had happened and reported me to the school principal.

Once again I was in trouble. It seemed that one way or another I would always end up in some kind of trouble. It was never proven that I had done anything, but the label was on me as being the drug supplier for the school.

Lesson #4
THE BEAUTY OF BOUNDARIES

- I spent my early years pursuing "Temporary Pleasure" that eventually leads to permanent pain. There is a saying that says "There is a way that seems right to a man…but the end is destruction."

- Some things feel good but the pleasure is only temporary. Drugs, alcohol, random sex, stealing, violence and cheating can give a temporary feeling of invincibility but our rehabilitation centers, prisons and insane asylums are filled with people who believed in temporary unrestricted pleasure.

- I eventually learned that every painting needs the boundary of a canvas in order to see it's real beauty. I discovered the beauty of boundaries only after going through unnecessary years of temporary pleasure from a life with no rules.

- Any game without rules is a game of chaos. Every basketball court or soccer field or football field has lines that mark out where the game is to be played. If the lines are removed or we play outside the lines the result is chaos.

Chapter 5

Living Large Part 2

As I grew older, I became more and more in charge of my school environment and was looked up to by others who were growing up. Many students feared me because of my reputation, but others looked to me as a hero. Younger guys in school used to try to imitate Davy B. Some would try to walk like me and others would wear clothes that they saw me wear. I got a lot of respect from the younger ones in school and in my community.

I remember times when I left from home to hang out at the University Of Warren Street and as I would pass the homes of young boys in the area, they would come running out just to say "What's up Davy B". Later I learned from these guys that they would actually get together as brothers and neighbors and talk about who they were going to be like when they grew up. The older guys on Warren Street were heroes to them. Some would say "I'm going to be like Davy B, or I am going to be like DC", others would say they were going to be like my brother, "Chimmy B" or "BB" or "CH" or others. Unfortunately, they did become like us and some later became a lot worse. Unfortunately that same story is repeated in neighborhoods worldwide.

One thing about being on the street is that you are obligated to maintain the reputation of your area wherever you go. People had to know that Davy B was from the UWS and had friends in Harlem. Whenever we went back on the blocks, we had to bring back a report of how we represented our neighborhood. This meant that we had to establish a reputation at school by whatever means necessary and protect that reputation by fighting or having all the girls or whatever it took.

It seemed like wherever I went I was always ahead of my time. I was almost always the youngest in the group, but was well liked and respected because I was smart and could operate around guys who were older than me. I can recall going into night clubs at age of 15 and friends who went with me who were 18 years old couldn't get in yet I could enter.

Our favorite nightclub at the University Of Warren Street was called the Banana Boat. This club was the "joint" back then; everybody who was anybody hung out at the Banana Boat. We used to hang out partying, drinking and having a good time until 3 or 4:00 a.m. in the morning, going from the club to one of the fast food joints that were still opened-either "Dirty's" or "Keith's Chicken Shack."

Back at school we had a group of guys, who would get together every lunch time to smoke weed and hang out. We chose an abandoned building in the bushes behind the school and we would all hang out there together during the lunch periods.

To be a part of this crew meant that you had to be from the street or a certified bad boy. None of these guys could sing in a choir or become a prefect or school president. The names told the story and each had a reputation. There was MM who famous for smoking more weed that humanly possible, KT from Harlem, FG from the Valley who was a famous bad boy known to fight at short notice, rob tourists sell drugs and do other things at night that need not be mentioned. MF from Mason's Addition, who was the brother of a famous Junkanoo leader in the Bahamas and a star athlete; SD, who was another bad boy from the Valley, and DM who was famous for smoking large amounts of marijuana.

There were many others who would come and go but this was the main crew. Sometimes one of us would be responsible for stealing lunch from the lunchroom while other times, we would buy lunch. This crew was known in the school as the official bad boy crew.

Around this same time the nightclub called Banana Boat sponsored a junior basketball team (under 18 years old) and I became a member. This team was pretty good on the court, but off the court we were terrorists. Our coach, Rudolpho, used to drive a bus and would pick up team members for practice. Unfortunately, we used the bus ride to terrorize people in neighborhoods as we passed. We would have all kinds of weapons on the bus and on the way to practice we would hit people who were walking on the sidewalk, beat them with mob sticks, dump water on couples who were walking down the street and whatever else wicked we could do.

The Jammers were an adventurous bunch. There were times when people who we had hit would remember the bus and throw rocks and bottles at us. Sometimes we would speed off and other times we would stop to fight.

On one occasion we got into something with some guys in an area called Yellow Elder and we got off the Bus with machetes, big chains, tire irons, rocks, bottles and whatever else and went to go after these guys. As we approached, we realized that some of the guys were friends of ours and we ended up not going through with the fight because one of the leaders of the area was a guy nicknamed "Bad T". "Bad T" was a close friend of BB and one of our other players, so we ended up laughing about it and moved on. Many years later both of Bad T's sons would end up being imprisoned for murder. I was a bad boy, but I didn't like causing indiscriminate trouble like some of my other friends. I was nice compared to them, they would go to events and take over and end up having to run because they beat up someone or fooled with someone's girl.

As time went on, my activities and schemes changed, but the trend was still the same. We have a bus system in the Bahamas called Jitneys and sometimes my friend, Black, who was actually from an area called "Kemp Road" but hung out on Warren Street, and I would get on the Jitney and when we reached our destination we just walked off and did not pay. When the bus driver complained we told him to come and get us. The bus drivers sometimes threatened us but we just laughed and walked or ran away.

On another occasion I needed a taxi so I flagged one down along with two friends American Sam and IV. The taxi driver thought he knew my parents so he asked me how they were doing and how my father's gas station was doing. I just went along with the program and acted like I knew what he was talking about. The others sat in the back seat not knowing what I was going to do but waiting on my cue. I didn't tell them I had no money to pay the cab fare so they didn't know what I was going to do. When we arrived near to our destination I told the cab driver to pull over. As soon as he pulled over I darted from the car and the other guys followed suit. The cab driver was stunned. He drove around looking for us and called the police. We were long gone.

Another time we were hanging out on Warren Street when I just decided to do something that came to my mind. I just decided that the next person who passed the corner I would hit them with a tree limb I was playing with. Sure enough the next car that came by, I let the guy have it right in his face. The car skidded off the road and he came roaring back. I don't' know why but it seemed I picked the biggest and meanest dude to hit in the face with a tree limb. He came back ready to tear off the person's head who did it and when he approached the group of us my friend 007 said, "I did it and what are-you going to do about it?" Of course 007 didn't do it but he was standing up to this guy in my place so I promptly picked up the largest rock I could find and slammed the guy just below his neck with this big rock. He stumbled a bit then ran off, got in his car and was gone.

After a while we forgot about it, but that afternoon as we were all sitting on the wall, this guy came back speeding by in his car. We saw him coming but didn't move right away until we realized he was trying to run us all down. We all jumped over the wall as his car ran right into the wall we were sitting on. Everyone scattered as he got out of the car with a shotgun and a big dog. He was steaming. I ran around the block and ran into a neighbor's house and hid in their kitchen. The neighbor called the police as I hid.

After a while we left and went back on the corner. While we were sitting there the police came and searched everyone for guns and drugs. They didn't believe it when we told them the neighbor had called the police because someone had chased us with a gun. They were convinced from past experience that we would never call as they used to come around periodically with dogs and guns to try and find us with drugs. They also knew that we had smashed police cars and hurt officers in the past.

Sometimes I worked in my father's grocery store. As I said before, wherever I went there was some kind of trouble. As I worked behind the cash register I would take some of the money from the cash register and put it in my socks. I changed the prices on goods so that I could earn extra money. I also sold drugs to my customers from the store. I would bring my bag of weed to work and stash it under the counter or in my socks. My drug customers would come and I would sell drugs right from the store.

Sometimes I would cuss out customers who argued with me about prices that I changed. They would say to me, "But that was $1.00 yesterday how come it's $2.00 today." I would tell them whatever I felt like saying, and eventually some of these people told my father what I had done. He didn't believe them at first, but one day a gentleman he respected came into the store and demanded that I serve him. The man asked me to show him where the meat section was and I pointed to it and told him where it was. He demanded that I leave the cash register and serve him. I promptly told the man F…….. you. He threatened to tear off my head but decided to wait until my father came. I had my machete under the counter and grabbed it. He looked at me and said the only reason he did not beat me badly was because he knew my father.

He waited until my father came and told him the whole story. I had gone out at the time. When my father returned he confronted me and was furious. He slapped me and I broke away and went outside and picked up two bottles to throw at him. He told me he was going to call the police and locked the door, he was in shock and wondering if I was high or what was wrong with me. I then left and ran back to Warren Street and hung out there. He told me not to come back home so I hooked up with my friend

Black from Kemp road and went to live with him.

My mother was asking for me to come back home and later when I went home to get my clothes I met my mother at the door crying, she pleaded with me not to go. Eventually she told me she would prefer that my father leave and I stay rather than me leave. I later returned back home as my father moved out.

Life at the University Of Warren Street had become an adventure in an amusing way. At the time, it was fun; my reputation grew after I fought my father. Some of my friends said "man you crazy, fighting your own father." We used to party all the time, every weekend hanging out in nightclubs and on the wall smoking weed or using cocaine. Many times we would just pack up in a car and search around the Island for parties whether we were invited or not. Sometimes this would cause fights, because we would go to parties and take over the bar at events which we were not even invited to.

Sometimes we had to run from parties because the police were after us. Sometimes we had to run from people shooting at us or throwing objects at us. I remember one occasion I was attending a party that we had crashed in an area called Sea Breeze. Perhaps the owners of the house or someone attending called the police about a group of us who were standing on the side of the house smoking weed. The police came up with dogs and guns and ran after us. I ran through several yards past guard dogs until I was safely out of their sight.

As I grew older I did more crazy things. Downtown Nassau is called Bay Street and on many days a group of us would go there and hustle money from people who passed by. We would hang out on Bay Street all day and stop people who passed by and ask them for money to buy lunch or a drink. At the end of the day you could make enough money hustling as you would from working on a regular job.

Anyway, one day we were on Bay Street hustling and the day was coming to an end. My friend Black and I were hanging out together. Black was extremely dark in complexion and I was very light skinned. We were like salt and Pepper but this was my friend and we used to do all kinds of things together. We were hanging near a store called Bonneville Bones when two guys we knew from an area called the Valley came to the store riding on some nice bicycles. Recognizing me, one of them asked if I could watch his bicycle. I said sure as they went upstairs. While they were upstairs Black looked at me and I looked at him and off we went on the guys' bicycles. They saw us and ran shouting at us, but it was too late. We later sold the bicycles.

My brother was still selling drugs and he would have suitcases and grocery bags of weed stored in our house. Sometimes my mother would find the weed and she would be so upset until she would cry. Sometimes my brother would move it out of the house only to bring it back later. No matter where he stored it, my mother would find the drugs; whether it was in the roof, deep in the closet or wherever, she would always find it. We used to say that my mother could work for the drug unit as a sniffing dog; she would always find the drugs.

I was not the main drug dealer but some of my friends in our area and other areas looked up to me as having a lot of drugs. I had all kinds of customers. DJ's at the local station, politicians, school teachers, you name it and they bought drugs. I thought I was cool, that I was really special but obviously there were many things I didn't understand. Although others looked at me and saw me as a bad boy or gangster, I never really saw myself as a really bad boy, I thought my friends and associates were the bad boys and I was sort of bad.

I never thought of myself as a violent person either. I didn't fight as often as my friends did and after a while I tried to avoid going some places with them because they liked to fight so much. I was athletic but skinny and although I studied karate, I really didn't like getting in fights like they did. Sometimes I look at the young guys I work with now and I think these guys are crazy; they are placing their lives in danger, they're killing one another. Then I look back and realize that I was just like them in some ways.

I can recall times when Warren Street ended up in a war with other areas. We used to fight with Rock Crusher over basketball games and other notorious areas including Bain Town. One night there was a party on our block and a fight ensued. Some of my friends beat this guy called Big G almost to death. They slammed him with a big rock, slapped him with a machete, beat him with a chain from a tow truck; he almost died and had to be taken to the hospital where I think he was for several weeks.

A few days later his boys came back and attacked us with guns, machetes and every other weapon you could imagine. I was not on the corner that day but I was sitting at home when my younger brother, Congo Bill came running into the house out of breath. He could hardly talk. I asked him what happened and he related to me how they came after him with a truck and he had to run through peoples' yards and through the bushes and just narrowly escaped. Fortunately all of our guys escaped although they did catch some guys who were from another neighborhood and beat them severely, though those guys insisted they were not from our area and they were not but they got what was directed at us.

After that incident we had a meeting. We drew up a battle plan and decided that if they came by truck we would throw Molotov cocktail bombs on the truck and as they ran, we would shoot at them and throw bottles and other weapons. After we had our plan together we waited for them. I stood on the corner with two machetes' and a chain used to pull cars and we waited for them to show up. My friend BB asked me to pick up his gun that was stashed away near the shack. It was a .38 or .44 but I could not find it where he said he hid it. One of the guys DK, whose father was a policeman and actually a bodyguard for a top government official, actually loaned us his gun. As I look back I can hardly believe that there I was in a position where I could kill or be killed, but that was life living large at the University.

Another time I remember I went to a public event with my friend BB who was always fighting and in some war or the other. We were hanging out in an area called Fort Charlotte where a lot of public events and concerts were held when all of a sudden we were surrounded by a group of gangsters from "The Bottom". I had forgotten that a few days earlier one of their guys tried to fight BB and he had picked up a baseball bat to beat the guy but the bat broke and about ten of these guys went chasing after BB but one of my other friends "Psycho" who always travelled with guns came by with a loaded shotgun and rescued BB who in turn started shooting at the group who scattered in the bushes. These were the same guys who now had us surrounded. Fortunately as they were about to attack us some of the guys from Harlem showed up at the same time and a confrontation was avoided. I remember walking away from that situation thinking that was a close one. As we left and went back to the truck we came on about four of the same guys saw us on the back of the truck and started to come our way, they know BB was crazy so as they came close BB picked up a steel pipe and I picked up a baseball bat but they kept walking because they didn't have any weapons with them

After I graduated from school I got a job working in a bank. From the moment I began working in the bank I caused trouble. My first order of business was to sell weed and cocaine to staff in the bank. Then I started stealing money through a fraud scheme. I was eventually caught but the lady who caught me promised not to tell anyone if I ceased doing what I was doing. Fortunately no one else found out about the scheme.

As usual I moved form one scheme to another. My next scheme was to use the bank's copy machine to copy money. Bahamian money comes in different colors and the tens and one hundred-dollar bills were dark blue. At night in the dark you could not tell that they were copied on a copy machine at least for a few minutes. So I copied the money on the copy machine and used it to buy drugs at night. I then passed some of the money onto my friends. We didn't worry about the police because we only used the money to buy drugs.

We would get in a fast car and go to the drug dealers on the street corner and ask for a bag of weed. We would then fold the money (because I only copied it on one side at times); present it get the drugs and speed off. My friends and I almost caused a serious war and ended up being wanted by drug dealers. They say when you are young you are stupid but I guess we didn't care because we did the same thing in a number of different areas in Nassau. Why I did this I really don't know, but it seems once you become an official hoodlum, you go from one thing to another without much thought. One level of evil to another!

I ended up in another bad situation when I sold drugs to the son of a well known Bahamian official. He had heard that I had some Colombian gold and so he came looking for me to sample some. He purchased an ounce from me and we went into the shack and were smoking the weed and talking. After a while when it was time to go I got up but he didn't move. I tried to pull him up but when he stood up he seemed disoriented. I didn't think anything of it at first, but I got concerned after I had to actually walk him to a neighbor's house and he was mumbling incoherently. I figured he would sleep it off so I left him at the gate of his cousin. The next day I got a call stating that the police were looking for me. The boy's parents had told the police I gave him the drugs and that I was a drug dealer. Fortunately they had no real evidence and I was able to evade a conviction. Unfortunately the boy never recovered. He ended up in the insane asylum and was on and off drugs for years before killing himself with drugs.

LESSON #5
PROGRESS IS MORE IMPORTANT THAN PERFECTION

- Sometimes we delay important decisions because we have flaws. We say I will wait until I become better to change. The reality is that we need to change in order to become better not the other way around.

- Perfection is elusive, progress isn't. None of us will be perfect but we can all make progress.

- Be diligent about making progress but be patient because even the best people in life go through periods of disappointment where they don't live up to expectations.

- Always remember that transformation is a process and not a one time thing. We can make a decision to change and become better but it can take some time for the actual transformation to take place.

Chapter 6

GIRLS GIRLS EVERYTHING

When it comes to relationships with the opposite sex, I could not in good conscience talk about some of the things I did when it came to women because I don't think it would serve any good purpose. Suffice it to say, I did some horrible things that I have repented for and I will only discuss some of the things I believe are relevant to my story.

Like most young men in the world, I was attracted to young ladies. And like most young men in the world I learned the wrong lessons about young ladies. After I had gone through my initial Sunday school training, my goal and intention was to follow the plan outlined by society. I liked girls and had "girlfriends" when I was very young, but as I grew older, my mind was twisted by the streets and my neighborhood, so I started to look at girls differently.

I heard guys talk about their experiences and how they were "feeling up" girls and having sex. As a youngster in elementary school, a few friends and I held court with the young ladies and spent much time talking boy and girl stuff, and sneaking a little kiss on the lips here and there; a hug or holding hands. This was preparation for the big day when we would find out the real birds and the bees story.

Some of us would do what many young men have done over the years like put a mirror on your shoe and stand near the young ladies to see what was under their dress. If that failed we would drop our pencil on the floor in class and kneel down under the desk near one of the young ladies to get a peek.

Though much of my learning about girls was not formal, the education from the street was my education. Nothing in Church was said about girls, but a lot was said in school. One of the first things I learned was that the pornographic magazines (Playboy etc) contained some interesting pictures. As was outlined earlier, we lived nearby a magazine distribution and in my quest to steal comic books I ended up stealing pornographic magazines that unnecessarily stimulated my interest in sex. I became addicted to pornography at an early age.

I heard nothing in Church about sex, so my street education was the predominant education when it came to women. My parents said nothing to me about sex, I don't remember Church leaders saying anything so just about everything I learned about women I learned on the streets. In my own little world I was in search of girls who wanted to have fun.

As I entered high school, the chase took on a new turn; the next phase was the touch phase. I moved from looking to touching. Being the bad boy that I was, whenever a young attractive lady sat next to me in class which was very often, I learned to get a feel. Rub her legs touch her behind whatever I could get to feed my testosterone driven sex drive.

My interest heightened when someone brought a book to school that several of the guys and girls read called the "Happy Hooker." This book had graphic tales of sex and debauchery; it was some nasty stuff. This fed my sex appetite further and lined up with the street culture. No matter whom you were, if you were on the street you had to be into girls. If you were homosexual in my area, you would get beat up or attacked in some cases even shot at. If a homosexual passed our block or we saw one, we would beat him badly because we detested homosexuals.

As I grew older, girls began to seek me out. In high school I had one girlfriend called 'India' who hung with me everywhere I went, even in detention after school. She used to take notes for me. She was my first real girlfriend. We stayed close for a long time but eventually I left her as I descended into the negative street lifestyle. Later there were a group of girls who all liked me. Although I was perceived as a bad boy in many ways, I was still a prime target when it came to girls. Many of the girls in my high school saw me as a prize. Looking back, it's amazing to see how many girls like bad boys. It seemed like the guys who were smart and doing well in school would hardly ever be the interest of the finest girls, so many of them seemed to gravitate to my type.

As was the story in so many areas of my life, my education when it came to the opposite sex was done on the corner from the perspective of the guys I hung with. I was the youngest so I took notes from the older guys. I learned how to go to the party or the nightclub and slow dance with older ladies. In fact, there were a number of girls who were older than me who used to seek me out at parties and nightclubs, because I was young and handsome and in some cases because they knew my brother who was even more of a ladies man than I was. Some of these relationships were not really as a serious love interest but more like a project. I felt comfortable with them too, because I didn't have anything to prove.

To the girls my age, I had to prove that I could handle myself but to these girls, I knew I was in school with them, so I just relaxed and learned. While I learned at this level about girls on the streets I learned another angle. When the guys were together on the wall at least one of us followed every girl that passed. We would say hello or ask for a phone number of throw out some kind of line to get their attention. If they didn't respond or acted like they were offended, we would cuss them out and say the worst things you could imagine. Some girls as you could expect, were afraid to pass our area after a while. Of course this only happened to girls who were not a part of the Warren Street scene. We protected the girls from our area. Often we would have contests or bets to see who could 'get' a particular girl first.

My whole education when it came to girls was all wrong. I learned to abuse girls when I thought I was being cool. I recall as a teenager, I was sitting on the corner and a group of us were talking about girls. I mentioned a particular girl I was going with and how she was special. One of the guys called DI, decided to give me an education about women. He had a can of soda in his hand and he started to drink it. He drank a little and said it was sweet; he drank some more and said it was sweet. When he was finished he crushed the can and threw it in the bushes. Afterward he told me that was how you deal with women; get all the sweetness you can get, and then throw it away when you are finished. He and some of the guys said if you paid too much attention to women, it would make you soft and cause women to take advantage of you. Some education I received.

While I was still in high school I met a young lady who was the sister of a young lady I had been friends with. I spotted her as we were about to go to a class beach party and we kind of hit it off. Later when we arrived at the beach and everyone else went in the water; I stayed near the music and the food because I noticed that this young lady was there. Using my 'training' as the music played, I put my lines together and some chemistry developed.

She was not living in Nassau although she was Bahamian. She lived in West Palm Beach. That summer we spent a lot of time together doing the things that teenagers do. She lived in an area called Masons Addition, that was a pretty rough area but I spent nights talking and walking around in her neighborhood. Sometimes we would find a secluded placed and get into normal teen sexual behavior. We became tight and it developed into a teen "love" experience. I walked and hiked rides to get there and back although it was a long way from where I lived. I would go to her house and stay there until late at night. I knew it was a dangerous area but I had friends in that neighborhood, so I didn't worry about it. I always carried a long 12" knife in my pocket because sometimes someone from my area or I might have done something and you never knew who you would meet.

One night I caught a ride with a guy who I didn't realize was a homosexual. When he was supposed to drop me off at my destination he asked me to take a ride with him. I cursed him out and let him know he didn't know who he was dealing with. I got so mad I was going to kill him. I pulled out my big knife and was going to stab him in his throat, but he stopped the car in fear and I exited. As he drove away I picked up some big rocks and threw them at the car. In spite of this I would still hike rides and even walk at night to my girl's house.

We talked about being together and even possible marriage and had a good time for a while. When she left, we exchanged letters and cards. Eventually my street manners did me in. She questioned the friends I hung around with and tried to get me away from the street and my bad boy friends. Unfortunately these were my 'homies' and that's how I lived so I wouldn't leave them alone. She kind of accepted me in spite of this.

Things were going well, but eventually we split after my street education of abuse got the best of me. She saved up her money to buy a gold watch for my Christmas gift, but I didn't even buy her a gift. She was so upset that when I came to see her, her mother told me I could not do so. I tried in vain, but she would not talk to me. I was devastated because I was really attached to her and did not mean to be ungracious with her during the Christmas Holidays. I was just careless and following the rules of the street and really not very thoughtful at the time.

That experience caused me to have a worse view of women than I did before. After that point I had no interest in love or relationships just a good time. Unfortunately several girls fell in love with me, but I had learned that there was no such thing as love. I went on a quest where I had relationships with girls younger and older than me.

All of the relationships were basically one way. Let's have a good time and don't get hung up on me. From week to week I did not stick with any one girl. Whoever was available on the weekend would be cool with me. I went with younger girls, older girls, married women and some who were much older than I was. A lot of my activities involved drugs, alcohol and promiscuous sex, but once again I was living large and didn't feel any remorse about it. Sometimes I would drive their cars and they would buy me presents but I never reciprocated. It got to a point where although on the outside I appeared to be a nice guy to young ladies (and deep down inside somewhere I still was) I had become wicked to the core.

Sometimes on the weekends I would go out with the girl who had the most money or the one with the car. I remember one girl who pleaded with me to go out with her and I replied that I couldn't go anywhere because I was broke. She assured me that she had money so I said okay let's go.

And I lived like this for several years. There were parties every week, girls, sex in the backseat of cars, on the beach at night, in the hotel, in an apartment somewhere on and on. Me and some of my friends used to frequent the hotels on the Cable Beach strip in Nassau and pick up foreign women, mainly American girls and get them high and "show them a good time". Unfortunately that lifestyle had its consequences and on two occasions it resulted in me having to go to the doctor to get medicine for an STD.

There are many things that I did that were a lot worse, but I don't think it would be helpful to include some of those details in this book. I could have easily gone to prison for some of the things I did but thank God I didn't. That was my life at the time and how I lived and kept on living. It seemed like a good time at the time the parties, the nightclubs the drugs and the girls, but time would tell a different story. I learned some other things that were really on the verge of criminality, in fact some of these things were criminal and my friends and I could have ended up behind bars for years as a result.

I remember one day we were hanging on the corner in Warren Street when a girl known as Samona, came to visit one of the guys alias G. As she was waiting for him a conversation ensued, D C and 007 traded some words with her about who could do what in bed. As the conversation went on DC and 007 picked her up like a log in broad daylight and carried her screaming down the road and into our shack and proceeded to rape her. All of us who were on the corner were laughing because we were saying she got what was coming. Afterwards NP, one of the guys and I went into the shack and pleaded with her not to go to the police. She was hysterical. Fortunately after a long time of talking NP finally convinced her not to go to the police and he took her home. I know it sounds crazy but that was life on Warren Street and that was how we dealt with women, obviously a distorted perspective.

Women were treated in different ways at different times. This was a part of my education. Suffice it to say that there are things in all areas of my life, which I regret and some of my dealings with females would definitely fall into that category.

There were other relationships that I was in that ended up with abortions, because I said I didn't want 'no baby'. At the time I wasn't thinking about whether abortion was right or wrong, I just didn't want any children. One married lady had assured me that she was protected and I took her word. When it turned out to be otherwise, of course I reacted negatively. She asked me for money to help with the abortion, but I told her the baby wasn't mine and she had to take care of it herself.

My final story about girls was one that I regretted the most. As I went to College, I went to chill out as they would say. Trying to get away and start a new life. The problem was like they say you can't change a man from the outside, or by just a change of location. Change has to be an internal thing and nothing had changed with me on the inside.

I met a young lady called 'D' from Detroit and we started talking and we hit it off. I made my move shortly after and there I was back on the same routine. We both agreed that love was not a priority, but before I knew it she was in love. I was practically living in her apartment or she lived in mine until one day, though we had agreed that we weren't falling in love, we both did to a degree. I moved into her apartment at first and we were living together like husband and wife, and I didn't realize that she had really fallen in love.

One day she asked me if I loved her and I stated that I wasn't in love and in fact that I didn't know what love was. She was devastated and upset. After we 'broke up', we ended up living together again. She moved into my apartment and we continued the relationship, though I had made the statement about love. She had apprehensions and told me that her mother had said if you live with a guy he wouldn't marry you, but we ended up just enjoying each other without discussing commitment.

We did have a lot of fun at the time, getting high together, partying and enjoying college life. We went grocery shopping and shoplifting together and did all kinds of dangerous things. We went on trips together to places like Panama City and had fun like young people did at the time. Later on as the story unfolds in the next few chapters, I ended up leaving without much warning or consideration. Unfortunately this was my distorted perspective at the time and what I had learned about girls and this was how I was living.

Fortunately for me I learned better in the years that followed, but this was a time of living dangerously. One thing that happened to me that I had to repair for future years was how I treated women. Most of my early education taught me nothing about being a gentleman, about consideration for the opposite sex, but as you will read later in this book, I learned the right way after I made some major changes in my life.

Lesson #6
VISION is BETTER THAN SIGHT

- The road to a bright future begins with a bright mental photograph of what the future is supposed to look like.
- Vision for Life is not dependent upon eyes or sight but rather vision. Sight requires your eyes to be open, vision does not need sight to see.
- Martin Luther King Jr.–Had a Dream, a vision manifest during his lifetime, but yet provided the blueprint for a whole race of people.

Chapter 7

PRELUDE TO COLLEGE

After working in the bank for a year, my sister, who was attending Oral Roberts University came home during the summer and encouraged me to come to the school. She brought the school yearbook and noted that they had a top-notch basketball team. I was an avid basketball and baseball player, and as I looked through the yearbook it all seemed very interesting. I started to consider it in my mind.

Her life always seemed to be good, not as exciting as mine but I was sometimes tired of everything. Even though my life seemed exciting, deep down inside there were periods when I was empty and longed for something, not knowing exactly what that something was. Sometimes I would party all weekend and at the end of it end up feeling depressed. I wondered from time to time what her life was like.

In the back of my mind I believed in God and wanted to change someday, but I could never fathom myself as a Christian because of the regular stereotypes of Christians not being cool and considered soft on the street. I had a reputation as someone from the street and being a Christian did not fit into that equation at all. How could I go on the streets at Warren Street and tell the guys that I was a Christian. I just could not fathom the thought.

My sister, Marilyn was. a true warrior. She didn't care what we were into on Warren Street, she was fearless. Of course everyone knew her, but she was so bold until some days she would take over our block and collect up all the little children in the area and have Church; teaching them the Bible and singing right on the street corner where we used to gamble and use drugs. We would just move to another area until she was finished. Most of the guys never went to Church but she would sometimes corner the roughest guys and 'make' them go to Church with her. So Marilyn convinced me to give it a try and consider going to ORU. I thought about it but did not act on it right away.

During that summer my friend, KF indicated that he was in College and invited me to consider going with him. To get into Oral Roberts University I needed to sit the SAT exam and I did. The problem at the time was because I didn't study and because I was smoking so much weed, my results were so bad the school or the testing people wrote back and asked if my native language was English. I then decided to go to school with KF. I was still using drugs; in fact every day was a day for smoking herb. KF and I smoked all the time and sometimes we did something we called "touring", meaning we would get a bag of weed and just drive around all night smoking and cruising.

I was still working at the bank at the time and though I had a good job, I would still sell drugs and use them. In fact I used to get high on the job. I used to keep cocaine in my office and snort cocaine to stay awake and alert while I worked. One night I got an ounce of weed from my brother, then KF and I decided to go touring.

I had already applied to North Florida Junior College and had been accepted so we were scheduled to go to school in a few weeks. That night we rolled up a big joint that we used to call "spliffs" and began our tour of the Island listening to the music and getting stoned. We did not know at the time, but one of his tail lights were out so as we toured Bay Street in downtown Nassau, all 'up in smoke' we were joined by a police car with lights flashing. At first we just lowered the joints and drove along slowly. They asked us to pull over; we couldn't stop because the car was full of weed so we just kept going. The cops kept flashing for us to pull over.

We had to decide what to do. So we decided to keep at a slow pace initially but the police now insisted that we pull over and began using their car police horn and loud speaker. KF was driving and he looked at me and said hold on because he was about to make a dash. We sped off with the police in hot pursuit and went in and out of little corners with the Police behind us.

While we were maneuvering I took the opportunity to shake the weed out of the bag it was in and let it blow away. I didn't want to throw the whole bag out the window since the police were close behind and they might find the bag so I just emptied the bag, or so I thought. Once we got rid of the bag we stopped and the officers instructed us that they would search the car. The car still smelt like weed so they knew we had some at some point in time. They searched and initially found nothing. I had the opportunity to run but decided against it because the drugs actually belonged to me so I could not leave my friend with the police so I stayed.

After their initial search they found nothing. Then they searched again. This time they found a tiny amount of drugs that I had stashed under the seat. KF told the officers that they had put the drugs there because they had already searched and didn't find anything. I argued with the officers too, that they put the drugs there. Of course we knew that we had put it there, but we still insisted. They placed us under arrest and put handcuffs on me and started to take me into the police vehicle.

My friend at this time made a dash to get in the car and get away and I ran for the passenger door. I was met at the door by one of the officers who locked the handcuffs on my wrist just as I was about to open the door. I was quickly grabbed and I didn't resist as he took me to the back seat of the car and locked the door.

My friend however let them know that he was not going anywhere. He refused to get out of the car and the officer had to struggle with him to get the keys to the car. When they finally got him out of the car they tried to handcuff him but he let them know that they were not putting handcuffs on him and he proceeded to wrestle with them. The two of them could not handle him; he was a tough customer, so they continued to struggle. One of the officers ran to his car and used his radio to call backups. Soon there were several cars there; it was just like a movie scene. They got both of us in the car eventually and we were carted off to the Police Station. At the station we were stripped of personal belongings and placed into a cell already occupied by two other men.

As soon as I was safely in my cell I requested of the officer to make a phone call. I wanted to call my brother to assist me and to let him know where I was so that he could move the grocery bag of drugs that he had in our house in case the police came to search the house. The officer told me to shut up because I was a prisoner. I then cussed out the officer and threw food and urine at him.

It was at that point that they called CID officers and threatened to put a beating on me. They actually took me out of the cell and handcuffed me, but the cell they were going to take me in to beat me would not open. They decided to leave the handcuffs on me to sleep with as punishment. They left me in the handcuffs but I figured out a way to get out of them and kept them with me until morning. When they came to let me make my phone call, I handed them the cuffs and they were amazed.

I did get to make my phone call and called my brother and tried to talk to him in code so he could move the drugs. I asked him to move the clothes (meaning drugs) but he didn't figure out what I was saying. Fortunately they did not search our house as they normally do, so we both escaped a long prison sentence for selling drugs. Thank God the whole scene ended with me getting off. KF was charged and convicted of assault in spite of the fact that his father was one of the Chiefs on the police force. I guess they tried to get him back for resisting arrest and because they did not find anything but the small amount of the drugs in the Car.

Before they let me go a female officer took me into her office and lashed out at me for being involved in this activity. She said I looked like a good boy and even though she could charge me for the small amount of marijuana that I was found with she decided not too. She said I could get six to nine months of prison time for possession. She also said if I was charged I could end up with a police record and never be able to travel again. She asked me to promise her I would stay out of trouble and she would let me go. I faithfully made the promise and I thanked her and assured her that I was not a bad boy and just happened to be in the wrong place. I left the lockup laughing to myself about it but I was happy.

A few weeks later KF and I were off to Florida heading to school. Once I got to the College, I actually made a commitment to do better but that commitment only lasted a few days. I was getting high all the time and partying and not paying attention to my studies. I did all kinds of crazy things. I ended up stealing from other students, breaking into the school's office and stealing exam papers, burglarizing other apartments in the area so I could furnish my apartment. I stole sofa beds and KF and I actually stole a stereo system from the school library. He had an oversized bag and we actually walked right out of the school library and took the stereo from them. I also stole other electronics that were in the Library. I broke into other students' apartments and stole stuff and sold some of the stolen goods and stored other stuff in the ceiling of my apartment.

One night one guy from Hawaii or some place in the Pacific approached my girl and threatened me. I kicked him in his groin and beat him with a tennis racket I had in my hand and then ran back to the apartment to call FK. We got some long wooden logs that they used for fences and went after the guy but several of his friends showed up. We jumped up on a wall with them below and held the logs to swing at them, but they ended up running away because they didn't have any weapons and we were known around the school as people you don't fool with.

The college experience in Florida was one experience after another, I could only call it my college "Daze". Even though people could go to jail for up to a year for shoplifting in that part of Florida, my girlfriend and I would go to the food store and get a shopping cart, buy $10 worth of canned goods, and steal all kinds of meat worth a lot more. What we would do is stuff the meat in her handbag and then put the hand bag at the bottom of the cart. When we went to the checkout counter no one would notice the hand bag at the bottom of the cart because it was blocked by the checkout register. We would then pay for the few small items and walk out the store with a bag full of expensive meat on the bottom of the cart.

When I wasn't doing that, I had the long trench coat that I would go shopping with at the convenience store. I would always buy one item, like a pack of cool aid, but as I was walking down the isle and checking the mirror I would be collecting spam, tuna fish, and corned beef and stuffing them into my trench coat. When I got to the register I would pay for the small inexpensive items and walk out with a coat full of canned goods.

Sometimes my girlfriend and I would go on a trip to a hotel and check in with a different name and then I would steal everything I could find in the hotel, the bed spread, lamps, towels, even the light bulbs. I would put them in my suitcase and take them to my apartment.

If I did go to a store I used to take my own price labels, put them on products and argue with the staff that they had the wrong price on items and they had to sell it to me for the price that was on it. I was supposed to be getting an education but I was working on the wrong things.

My friend KF was even crazier than me, and we did all kinds of things. I remember one occasion I had to rescue one of the Hawaiian guys from getting killed by KF. We were in KF's girlfriend's apartment when this Hawaiian guy came in and asked where the girls were. I cussed him out and told him to get out before he got hurt. He stood there half drunk and didn't move right away. KF picked up a big knife and went to stab the guy. I was scared for him and grabbed him and shoved him out the door and kicked him before KF could get to him.

One of the potentially worst experiences of my early college years was when I decided that I needed a gun. Up to this time KF and I did not have had a gun. I had seen some people in the area that I believed I could rob and I started to think that no one would ever expect a college student to be robbing people, so I thought I could get away and no one would figure out. I decided to steal a gun that I saw. A man from the area pulled into our apartment complex and he had three guns in his truck. I informed KF and we decided to steal the handgun and leave the shotgun. After KF broke into the guy's truck, I took the gun and hid it away in the back of an old building in the bushes so we could retrieve it when needed.

About two days later I got a call from my girlfriend and she was frantic. She said they locked up KF and they were looking for me. I told her to pack some of my clothes in a suitcase and I was going to skip town and head back to the Bahamas, I didn't want to go to jail in Florida. I then hid out in another apartment preparing to leave town. Later on that day or the following day she came back to me with a message from KF that the Sherriff's Department was willing to work with the school on a deal for us, so we wouldn't have to go to jail. I had not prayed or gone to Church in years, but I prayed that night. I asked God to help me get out of this situation and I promised to change my ways.

The next day KF and I showed up at the school for this meeting with the Sherriff and the Dean of the School. The Dean had already talked with us and he let us know the school was willing to work with us and we would end up on probation that would not show up on our transcript if we kept clean for three months. I was feeling better but KF and I got a shock when we were waiting for the Sherriff. The meeting was supposed to be with the Dean and the Sherriff, but while we were waiting there for the Dean he did not show up and only the Sherriff did.

Up to this time the Sherriff had not seen me, so I started to think they just wanted to get the two of us together so they could lock us up. I looked at KF and he looked at me when we saw the sheriff coming down the walkway with hand cuffs in his hand and we started to think about running. We talked about it but decided that the Sheriff might have been genuine so we stayed. The Sherriff came and talked to us and said he understood that as young men sometimes we make mistakes. He said he thought we were good young men, who had made one bad decision and he was willing to work with us. He asked me to turn in the gun and the school would oversee our probation, so it would not become a criminal matter.

I almost blew the deal the day before because when they asked me for the gun, I told them I didn't know anything about a gun. There was a witness who had seen me with the gun so I was really making a foolish decision, but I was able to correct my mistake.

When I got out of that situation I could only say thank God, if not because of my prayers then my mother's prayers. I had not told her about what was happening but as always she was praying for me. Many times she would tell me she was praying for me and that something was wrong even when I had not told her anything. So it seemed she was much better in touch with God than me. Maybe I reached God indirectly, through my mother. The end result was that my wish was granted. I was off the hook. God did his part and I started to think I needed to do mine.

I recall the time when I was involved in another police chase and getting locked up that my mother told me something had caused her to get up at 4.00 a.m. and pray by my bedside. It was the same time that the chase was going on, when she told me that I thought to myself this is some kind of Miracle, how would my mother know what was happening and why would she get up and go by my bed and pray.

Some of these occurrences caused me to think there must be a God, but I guess because of my background I could not bring myself to say I would give my life to Him and become a Christian. When I thought about being a Christian I felt I could not do without the ladies, the drugs and the wild parties that I had become accustomed to. I guess I told God thanks but I can't handle the whole deal now, give me some time to work until I get to that point.

My way of paying back for my part of the deal was to send home to Nassau for a record that I had heard a few months earlier by someone, who I did not know but, who would cross my path later and in fact, we would become partners in ministry. A ministry I had no idea I would be involved in. The name of the song was BRAND NEW WORLD by a group called the Visionaries, and Myles Munroe was the leader of the group.

I was still shacking up, smoking Colombian Gold and snorting coke, but every Sunday I would put this record on and just listen to the words while I was high. The words stated "We don't like the way the world is turning, something inside us always yearning, yearning for a brand new world. People everywhere are so confused, leaders don't know just what to do; everybody wants a brand new world. "But if you want a brand new world, you gotta have a brand new people, if you want a brand new people you gate have a brand new life, if you want a brand new life you gat have a brand new spirit and if you want a brand new spirit you gat come to Jesus Christ."

That song was sung as my Church many Sundays, I guess my way of telling God I know you are there and one of these days we will get together. I can't accept everything now but sometime Lord, sometime later I would make that change.

My second down payment to God if you can call it that was when I sent my application to Oral Robert's University. I didn't tell my girlfriend or any of my other friends in College or at home because I felt that if I did people would think I was freaking out. So I kept it to myself. I thought in the back of my mind that if I went to the school my sister attended with the Christian background it had perhaps it would help me to change and get away from the lifestyle I was living at the time.

When I had first applied as I noted previously, I really didn't qualify. The school's standards were high. They wanted you to be a born again Christian; they asked questions like, "Did you use drugs or alcohol and were you sexually active." To every question on the paper I lied. I figured if I said the truth I would never be accepted, and if they knew my background they probably wouldn't accept me. Almost everything I said was not true. To complicate matters, I was now on probation and still cohabiting with a young lady.

Somehow to this day I can't figure out how I was accepted. Perhaps it was because of my mother's prayers. She, too, believed that if I could just get away from my environment I might change. Looking back, I can see the seeds my mother planted in my life. No matter how late I would be out at night, she would come to the room door and ask if I was going to Church. She would stay up late at night sometimes waiting until I came home even if it was 5:00 a.m. in the morning. She never gave up on me.

Somewhere deep down inside I felt I would make a change, but I didn't have the courage to do so. In the middle of my second term in College, I went to my mail box one morning not expecting anything in particular, but that morning would end up being one of the turning points in my life. Among other items in my mail I noticed a letter from Oral Roberts University. I had expected a reply from the school, but I knew the position I was in and didn't know if I would be accepted.

Would a Christian school accept someone who was on probation? There were doubts in my mind. As fate would have it or perhaps as my mother's prayers would prevail, when my transcripts were sent off my probation was not included in my school records. I was accepted into the school. I was to report to school in August of that year.

I was happy and yet confused. I did not tell anyone. My girlfriend and I had already discussed transferring to Miami Dade together and my partner and his girlfriend would also do the same. I felt I had to tell someone so I told him. He didn't quite understand but listened anyway. I told him not to mention it to anyone. He agreed. So I spent the rest of the semester studying, although not nearly as hard as I should or could have. I was still partying and having a good time, smoking weed, but in my heart I was trying to make a change.

LESSON #7
YOU BECOME WHAT YOU FOCUS ON

- Whatever preoccupies your mind is what you become. "As a man thinks, so is he!"

- Check your thoughts and interest and they predict your destiny.
- If you want a new destiny you need to have a new focus or you need to renew your focus.

- We were all designed by our manufacturer and ultimate father to be a reflection of him and his design. If we were ultimately born to be like God we will only become like God if that is our focus.

- Remember that to renew means to make new again. Sometimes we need to remember what we were supposed to be and re-focus on that rather than who we are now.

CHAPTER 8

THE MOMENT–THIS IS IT!

After a year full of excitement, fun, trials and questions, I came home after completing my first year of College. That summer I went back to work at the bank that I used to defraud, but I had toned down my act a lot. I hadn't changed but I was a little more subdued. I still spent my days and nights on the corner, partying and hanging out with my boys. Again, I almost ended up in trouble running from the police and selling drugs, but deep inside I was searching and longing for something better. So after a summer of partying and hanging out I decided to leave the Bahamas and go to Tulsa, Oklahoma the week before school opened.

That morning, before I left Nassau, I put on my clothing, Gangster hat, dark shades and left for the airport. My mother was so happy see me leave. Sometimes parents don't want their children to leave or they may have sad feelings about them leaving, but this was different. I don't know if in her mind she was saying, "Thank you Jesus," but I suppose I must have been thinking the Lord had come through again. I was going somewhere where the God to the universe could get my attention. I had no intention of becoming a Christian. I knew where I was going, but I was thinking in my mind about a change of environment and not becoming a Christian. I felt like it would be better for me if I was in another environment, but I just could never see myself as a Christian.

On the flight I just chilled and thought about life, reflecting on the summer that had just gone by and wondering what was ahead. I was actually supposed to be in Miami at this time. My girlfriend from Detroit had just called me a day or two earlier and although she was totally upset with me for what I had done to her, she had asked to see me before I went to Tulsa. We were actually talking on the phone and she was about to give me her address when the operator discovered that she was making a kind of illegal call and she had to hang up. I never got the address; she didn't know I was on my way to Tulsa.

As the plane touched town in Tulsa, my brother-in-law, Robyn Gool came to meet me. We had met briefly before but did not have a relationship. In fact, when I first met him I was thinking he was a nice guy, but not someone I would want to hang around. When he had come to Nassau for his wedding, his uncle who stood in the wedding was like me and my brother; so we got Uncle Eddie high on drugs and my brother and I were actually plotting to spike the punch at the wedding with alcohol to get everybody drunk. None of my sisters drank and most of the people at the Wedding were Christians, so we were just doing it to be wicked.

When I stepped off the plane he greeted me and I'm sure he recognized me and probably said to himself I wonder where this guy came from. I looked like a gangster. I didn't say much when we met other than the regular stuff but he knew what I was into. He also let me know he was not into what I was into. He said he knew guys who were like me but said he didn't hang around people like that but knew about them. We talked some more about basketball and what life was like in Tulsa. I just kicked back and relaxed.

I was glad to see my sister and we hugged as we arrived at the modest apartment where they lived in Tulsa. Their car was not at all fancy; they were not rich by any extreme. On my first night there, I felt like I was in a strange world. I didn't know where I was. I almost immediately noticed some strange things about them. I noticed that on their refrigerator they had a sign that read, "My God shall supply all my needs according to his riches in Glory by Christ Jesus." and the Scripture that it was taken from was placed under it. What that meant I would find out as time went on.

After a day or two in Tulsa, I realized Robyn was not working. Some mornings we would get up early and go to the Tennis court where he would teach rich white people to play tennis. Either that day or a few days later I heard them talking about a bill that needed to be paid and they acted as if they had no anxiety, though they did not have the money. It was at this time that I would learn what that Scripture meant.

One night we went to the grocery store and as we arrived home the money had still not come in for the bill, so quietly I wondered in my mind what they were going to do. When we opened the door there was a $100 bill under the door. I wondered who would come along and just leave a $100 bill under someone's door, so I asked. My sister explained to me that they didn't know who it was that left the money; they just believed that by their trusting God, he would provide for their needs.

The Scripture then came clear in my mind. My God shall supply all my needs! God must have sent me there at that place and time just to see that. I made a mental note of this event in my mind and went on about life. At this time, my sister had not too long before had her first baby, a boy whom they named Johms.

I always loved basketball, so when Robyn asked me if I would like to play ball I jumped at the opportunity. We hopped in the car and went to a local gym to play and we played with some of the guys there and very quickly I learned something about my condition. You see I smoked weed just about every day, I had spent most of the summer in nightclubs, partying and having what most people call a good time. I didn't realize how out of shape I was until he challenged me to a game of one-on-one. I was so tired I was about to drop.

This Christian guy beat me up in basketball, and while I was on the sideline almost out of breath, he proceeded to tell me some things about God. Meeting Robyn Gool and spending time with him was the most important meeting of my life up to that time. That meeting seemed preordained and resulted in a major challenge to my thinking. I realized there was something different about him, but I guess this also was a part of a larger plan God had for my life. He was not at all like me, yet he was a strong male. He could hang on the basketball court.

I didn't know too many Christian guys who could hang with anything. In fact I hated Church because I could never picture myself hanging out with the nerds I saw. In my mind, Church guys were too soft. Robyn was not like that. He was tough but he was a Christian and had strong principles.

Later during that week I went with them to my first Bible study. Now I hadn't been to Church in many years so I felt a little out of place. What would I be doing in a Church? I was expecting some weird looking people, who studied the Bible because there was nothing much else for them to do in the regular world.

There were only a few people in the Bible study, but the tone of their conversation was so happy. It almost seemed as if they were on drugs. They were talking about God and His blessings and how good He was and stuff like that. The songs they sang were happy. They seemed like some strange, but happy people. Then they started to "share" stories about what God had done for them. I listened and wondered what this was; I had not experienced this type of thing before.

In the Church where I grew up, people were nice but they seemed like they were just waiting to get to heaven and hoping to survive life. They used to apologize for singing, cry all the time, talk about God please take them home from this horrible world. I had never seen happy Christians with a positive outlook on life.

We kept playing ball and talking. Other strange things happened. When their young baby was sick they prayed for him before taking him to the doctor and sometimes they didn't have to go to the doctor anymore after they prayed. This too was strange to me. I didn't quite understand but I said these people are different. This stuff seems so real. They used to listen to teaching tapes and one of the guys on the tapes used to always say things like, "This is the day the Lord has made I will rejoice and be glad in it, this is a wonderful day and so on." Sounded like he was a little crazy to me, but it inspired me. How could someone be so positive about life? I later learned that the guy's name was Kenneth Copeland.

After more playing ball, Bible studies and going to the bowling alley, I began to wonder about this strange world I was living in. The more I talked to Robyn the more I started to wonder about my life. I listened to the stories about God and how He had this better life for me and I wondered about it. Robyn would explain some of the Bible to me that I did not understand, but I still didn't feel like I would become one of them. My world was too different. I thought I couldn't give up on the ladies and suppose I want to smoke weed sometime. I thought I could not be a Christian. But the questions would not go away.

As each day went by, I felt stranger living in their house. I felt like they were from one planet and I was from another. I also felt like the life they were living was better than mine. They seemed so clean, so free. I had a lot of time to think and I felt like someday I might find what they found. All of a sudden questions began to enter my mind. Could I make it as a Christian; was there really a God? The more I thought about it, the more I could not come up with who I was or why I was here on this earth. But I kept feeling the same as I did from a youth that there must be a God. Life just couldn't have happened; there must be someone out there. But I was not ready to face Him. So as I did many times before, I put it off and said I will settle this issue later.

Well 'later' ended up not being as late as I first thought. I went to another Bible study, then another, and another. By this time, I was beginning to enjoy these Bible studies, but I did not let them know. I just sat and listened, and checked things out. As they usually did that day, they lifted their hands in worship to God and sang these beautiful choruses and studied the Bible. Then they opened the meeting up for testimonies. They went around in a circle. Number one, "I thank God for blessing me, this week on my job. I got a promotion that I was praying for". Number two was another story of overcoming a difficulty and God helping out or believing that it was God. Number three, same thing. Number four, same thing. Number five. Number six. This was getting close to me it looked like they were going to call on me so I started to feel a little strange. They did call on me. "My brother, tell us what the Lord has done for you or helped you with this week". Most of my life I never heard of the Lord doing things for you this way. Sisters and brothers would get up and talk about how the Lord saved them years ago, but surely he hasn't had much to do with them since that time. "I don't have a testimony was my reply." They thought I was one of them so everybody kind of looked at me like, no testimony, where have you been lately? My brother in law Robyn stepped in and stated, "Don't worry about him he will have a testimony soon." I thought to myself, thanks bro, I will have a testimony? Maybe he knew something that I didn't know.

As the days went by without the influence of friends I really had time to think and the more I thought about it, the more I felt I needed what my sister and brother in law had. When I looked at my life and compared it to theirs, what they had seemed so free, so right. I enjoyed hanging out with the guys, partying, the girls, the drugs, but something on the inside said this was not right; there was a better way.

I don't believe either my sister or my brother in law expected things to happen so quickly. I didn't even expect things to happen so quickly. Looking back it seems like God arranged the whole thing. If I had not left home early then I would not have had the opportunity to talk extensively with Robyn or see what I had seen. After I entered ORU, I realize that if I had not seen what I had seen earlier it may have taken a lot longer.

After being in Tulsa a few weeks it was almost time to go to school. Robyn and Marilyn used to help out a preacher who had a little Church in a housing project in Tulsa, Oklahoma on the black side of town, called the Commanche Project. Only a few of the persons in the housing project came to Church on a Sunday morning. I kind of wondered in my mind why would they be going to this little rinky dinky Church. Then I realized they were givers; they were planting seeds of hope into lives that may not have normally been impacted by Christians. After all how many

Churches go into depressed areas to reach those who need to be reached?
The questions of that week were still stirring in my mind as I got ready for Church. I began to feel like Dave your time has come. It's time to give it up and make a change for the better. The Spirit was dealing with me as I entered the little room where the Church Services were held. I really don't know if I heard much of what was said that day. I really wasn't listening to the preacher. There was a war going on inside me between the Holy Spirit and my flesh. I felt on the one hand like man you need to get saved. On the other hand, I thought what would the guys back home think about me, how I could go home and say I'm a Christian. I also knew what the Bible said about sex outside of marriage being wrong, but here I was a young man sexually active for years thinking to myself if I become a Christian this means no girls at least in the way I had been dealing with girls for a long time. I kept thinking to myself I can't live up to that standard, so I postponed the decision in my mind saying I will wait until later.

I sat in the Service a little longer; all this time the battle was going on inside my head. "Do it now," a voice on the inside said. Then I heard, "Not today, you better take your time. These two voices kept coming to my mind over and over again during the Service. Finally, I decided to think about it some more and delayed my decision for another day.

The Service had ended and the pastor was about to give the Benediction when something on the inside, something so strong just rose up in me and I made that conclusive decision. In a moment I thought about all my reasons for delaying and I began to realize that if there was truly a God and if He did have a plan for my life, I had better trust Him rather than worrying about what my friends felt or what might happen with the girls. I decided this was too important to put off so without an Altar call or actually after the Altar call had ended, I stood up and announced to the preacher, I want to do it. He was a little surprised; in fact he was a lot surprised. He asked me what I wanted to do. I said, "Get saved or get right with God." It was such a shock to him that it took a few moments for everything to come together. Robyn and Marilyn also appeared to be a little surprised. I don't believe they thought I would change so soon. They did not even know the impact their lives were having on me. I knelt down said the sinner's prayer and that day I received Jesus Christ as my Lord and Savior.

LESSON #8
ANTICIPATE ADVERSITY, EXPECT TO OVERCOME

- You will never escape adversity. No amount of Money, fame, pleasure or privilege will exempt you from adversity. The rich and the poor are the same when it comes to adversity, there are rich people who go through problems that money cant solve and there are poor people who go through problems that lack of money cant solve.

- Every champion has built their reputation on overcoming adversity. We only remember winners and the greatest winner stories are those of persons who have been on the brink of elimination or desperation but fought their way through to victory.

- The Bible tells us that we overcome by "blood and testimony". A testimony requires you to pass a test.

- Jesus said (Matt 16:33) 'These things I have spoken unto you, that in me ye might have peace. In the world ye shall have tribulation: but be of good cheer; I have overcome the world.

CHAPTER 9

THE COMMITMENTS

It has been said that sometimes serving the Lord is not easy. Sometimes it's true and sometimes it isn't. Almost immediately after my prayer in that little Church, I started having doubts. I wondered if I was really changed. I expected something spectacular. I wondered if this was all there was to it. Thank God for my sister and brother in law. They assured me that everything was fine and that the Lord had indeed changed me and that I was on the right track.

As I began my studies at Oral Roberts University, it was culture shock. I was in for the biggest culture shock of my life. I had not been used to the American culture especially White American, and this school was basically a White school. I was more ignorant than prejudiced, but my first day and days were interesting. I wanted a room alone, not realizing that they normally insist that you have a roommate. Through my own maneuvering I ended up in a room by myself. I must admit, I had given my life to the Lord, but initially, this new life was a challenge for me.

My first week in school was okay but I learned some lessons about life as a Christian that I did not understand at first. I used to play basketball a lot and so I went to the school gym to shoot some hoops. I really didn't know anyone at the school and I didn't think anyone knew me. They could not tell there was something different about me or that I had come from a different background than the average student. So I joined a pickup game and started to play.

I guess the guys who were playing saw me as a new student and decided to intimidate me. They probably looked at me and said we can push this skinny guy around. They ran me through a pick and one guy stuck me real hard with a forearm. Well where I come from you don't mess with us like that. I thought in a Christian school something like this wouldn't happen so without any further conversation I told the dude I would xxxxxx him up right now and I went outside to get a piece of wood to beat him in his head. It didn't matter to me that he was much bigger. One of the other students, who I had met a few days earlier came running and pleaded with me not to do anything because I might get kicked out of school. I left the basketball area feeling like I had just let God down. I wondered if I could really be a Christian.

Fortunately a young lady friend of mine, who I had also recently met came to me and explained that because you make a mistake God is not going to turn against you and she noted that everything was okay. Later I asked the Lord to forgive me but I learned the lesson that walking with God is a process, you will make mistakes and you have to ask him for forgiveness and move on.

In the meantime I was learning more about this new life. Robyn would often pick me up on weekends and we would go on the north side (Black side) of town to play ball and at night we went to Bible studies. It was very strategic that he was there as I began to learn that not everyone at a Christian school is a Christian. The fact that he was there, and he and Marilyn encouraged me in the faith meant that I was beginning on a good foundation.

They would give me books to read and tapes to listen to and almost every Sunday I went to Church with them. I guess this was God's way of preparing a nursery school for me as a baby Christian.

As I stated earlier I learned very early that not everyone at ORU was a Christian. There were a lot of adjustments for me to make also. I had just come from a life of little or no discipline and here I was in a school where you had to wear a necktie, attend Chapel, go to Church on Sunday morning and follow so many rules that I had not followed since I was a little boy. But this was good for me. I needed the discipline and gradually I learned to adjust.

I learned to adjust to a lot of things. I learned to adjust to people walking around saying, "Praise the Lord," guys hugging, people quoting the Bible. I stood off from that "Christian Culture" for a while. Guys would come to hug me and I would tell them not me, I don't hug guys. I will hug the ladies, but not guys. Even though I loved the Lord and was happy in my new life, I still could not get into the mainstream of the Christian groove.

One of the things I learned was that many of the students at the school were not Christians, and in some cases were eagerly trying to go where I had just come from. Many of my habits had not changed, so I did some strange things during those initial weeks. One day during Open House, where male and female students are allowed to go into each others dorms for a period of time, I went with a group of guys into the girl's dorm. The young ladies were greeting the guys and this one young lady was kind of playing with me. Because of my previous habits I spontaneously grabbed her and pulled her into the closet in a joking fashion and pretended I was going to kiss her but didn't. The guys with me looked at me as if to say, "Hey this guy knows how to handle women, so let's hang with him." So they started to talk to me about going to some swinging parties and nightclubs but I quickly told them I was not into that, I had just come out of that scene. More temptations would come as time went on however. All this time I was growing steadily, making mistakes but I was growing. One Friday night Robyn invited me to a Bible study. On that particular night they were talking about the Baptism of the Holy Spirit and speaking in tongues. Robyn had indicated to me that Salvation was only the beginning and that there was much more to come.

I had seen people speaking in tongues and had known about it for some time as every now and then in my Church, as a young boy people would periodically speak in tongues and prophesy. I did not have a clear understanding of it however and just thought of if as something out there that was done by some Christians. He began to explain to me that this Baptism in the Holy Spirit was necessary as it was something that Believers in the early New Testament automatically did as with Baptism in water. He indicated to me that the purpose of this Holy Spirit Baptism was for power and through tongues or what he termed the prayer language you would edify yourself in God, and you could pray in a language that God understood even if you did not.

At this time I was excited about being a Christian and glad for the change in my life. I wanted more and that Friday night at a Bible study a gentleman, whom I did not know, prayed for a number of people and as he laid hands on me I felt something that was a little hard to describe. I felt light; there was a sensation in my stomach and shortly afterward I began speaking in tongues. As time went on, I began to read up more on the Baptism in the Holy Spirit and the Biblical basis for it. At that time I was very excited to be progressing in my walk with God.

Now I will be the first to admit that I was not perfect. I did my best to grow and I was growing, but I made my share of mistakes. In spite of the mistakes, I knew I was not turning back. Every now and then someone would get on my nerves and I would react the wrong way. There was no tag on me that said there was something different about me. So many times people did not realize that in my head there was this notation, "Don't mess with me."

One day some guys played a prank on me and put a roll of toilet tissue in my dryer. Now I was not the type of person who was into these stupid games as I saw it, so I promptly got a clothes iron from my room and went after the guy who I thought was responsible. He confessed and I told him and the other guys in my dorm area, don't be messing with me.

At different times I would cuss people out when I got angry or do something that was not in keeping with the Word. One time I picked up a bottle and rock and told this guy who was about two times my size that I would xxxxx him up today if he threw a snowball at me. He looked at me as if I must be crazy and walked away. I was still growing but I was going to slam him in his head if he threw the snowball at me.

I did other things from time to time that were not the best thing for a Christian to do, but like I stated earlier, in spite of it all I was growing. The funny thing is that girls and guys would come to me from time to time and try to get me to take them to a nightclub. Some even wanted me to get them some weed to smoke or do something out of the way. I tried to stay away from them, but because I felt like I could not hang with what I thought to be 'goofy' Christians, who were saying praise the Lord all the time I kind of stood in the middle.

After a good year in school, I did well in my grades and grew as a person; it was time to come home for the summer. It was time to test my commitment. During my first year my sister and brother-in-law were always there to keep me on track. Robyn became like my big brother. We would play ball together with some of the former ORU basketball players around Tulsa and every Sunday he would pick me up for Church. One thing I noticed about him was that he never wavered in his faith. Most of the players we played with were not Christians, but he was and did not let anyone influence him or change his stance.

I went everywhere with Robyn. Sometimes it was some rinky dinky Church in towns like Chickasaw or Cushing. He was also a pastor in the AME Methodist Church and so as he went around ministering in Churches I would always go with him. This was an experience that helped me a great deal, but also made me cynical about certain aspects of the 'Black Church'. There were all kinds of characters in some of these Churches. I had just gotten saved and I expected Church to be a 'Christian' place. Often the deacon would come outside to smoke a cigarette, the girl in the choir wanted my phone number; it seemed like many of these Churches never read the Bible because the Church seemed like a social meeting place rather than a place of worship.

I learned to take it in stride and learned that not everything that had the word, "Church" on it or not everyone who said they were a Christian were actually saved or living right. Some of my encounters were a test of faith. Every now and then I felt like pursuing some of the females who were interested in me but I decided not to do so, because I really wanted to live right and learn about God and his plan for my life. I passed up a lot of what I would have previously considered good opportunities.

That first year of college was a growing experience for me. There were ups and downs as a Christian, but in spite of all the complexities, I was steadily growing. I kept reading my Bible, praying and learning the Word as time went on. I did some crazy things during that first year of school, but much of it was just a part of me ironing out my growth as a Christian.

I remember sitting in Class questioning my teachers on what was wrong with Communism and thinking how they must have wanted to save me again. I had been reading a lot of Mafia and Black Panther books a couple years earlier, so I had some strange philosophies in my mind at the time. I also remember telling one of my teachers, as we looked at slides of the 'Holy Land', that I didn't see anything Holy about it. It looked like desert and dirt to me. Some of the other students thought I was 'different', some thought I was a Muslim. Most didn't know me however; they were forming their judgments on perceptions passed along from one to another. I still had a lot of rebellion in me that the Lord was working out. I still was not a nice person if I thought someone was messing with me.

After that first year at ORU, I came home and my first stop was back in the Hood. The 'University Of Warren Street". These were my homeboys; we were family in our own kind of way. I was welcomed back but there were some reservations. DI and SQ welcomed me and we began to talk. I stated that I was a Christian and that my life had changed. Their reaction was typical. DI said, "Man, why do you want to close your mind out to the world?" SQ said, "Man you can't be a Christian; you have already done too many evil things in life." He said God didn't want me. I tried to get them to understand, but I realized that while they sympathized with me they really couldn't understand. Later during the course of the next few weeks, I met the other guys and got the same reaction. Some couldn't believe me; others joked about it and questioned me. Some said I needed a good screw and that would take care of me; others offered me cocaine

or weed. I passed on all these opportunities and just stated my position that I was a brand new man.
Funny thing is and I have said this over and over again, how do you just wake up one day and say, "I am going to change my friends." It is a good thing to do, but it is often not that easy. These were the only guys I knew and the University was my hangout. And Church was a strange place. I was welcomed at Church almost like a hero. Many people were amazed at my 'testimony'. People were glad to see that I had been saved, especially the adults who knew me when I used to go to Church. Most of them had not seen me in years and I guess one way or another they had heard about my problems from my mother or others.

So Church was very nice and cordial to me. I felt that I should get some new friends, but the minute I began to hang around the 'Church' people, I felt like I was on another planet. It was strange. I felt I had entered a time warp; this seemed to be the largest collection of nerds in one place that I had ever experienced. There was such a difference in where I had come from and where they had come from. They could not see anything wrong, but I felt really strange around them. I ended up staying pretty much to myself after that and periodically hanging with the Church people, and other times I would go back to the street though I didn't participate in their activities.

After a period of hanging out on the blocks or in the Hood, I began to realize that I could not really make it in that environment. My friends did not exactly understand what I was going through and too often we got into religious arguments. They would kind of make fun of me by asking crazy questions, but I did notice that whenever we were one-on-one, it was a different story. One-on- one, they would say things to me like, "Davy B, that's a good thing what you have done but I'm not ready for that right now."

One of the toughest scenes I went through was not too long after I had returned from school. I was sitting in my living room reading my Bible when one of my old friends knocked at the door. MC was Mr. Party man. We used to smoke a lot of weed together, listen to music and party with the ladies. He had heard I was back in town and had come to the house with some weed. He looked at me in a very gleeful way and said, "What's up, you back in town, I gat some stuff for you." As he was talking and laughing I didn't smile, I just kept my Bible open and he began to realize that something had changed. So he asked, "So what's happening, what you into?" I pointed to the Bible, and said, "This is what I'm into." A part of me felt stupid talking about being into the Bible in the back of my mind I was thinking of all the good times and knowing that my 'homie' came looking for me so we could have a 'good' time together.

The room went almost like someone had died. I stated my case, that I was now a Christian. He didn't know what to say. He started to walk off and said, "Good to see you, take care man, we'll catch up later." It was years before we would get together again. It was difficult, but deep down inside I knew I had made the right decision.

As time went on, I realized it was time for me to leave so my visits to the old neighborhood became less and less. I began hanging by myself more and more. But I didn't care. I had made a commitment and I knew it was not only the right thing to do, it was the best decision. In fact, it was the only decision that I could make to better my life.

LESSON #9
THE ART OF REPLACEMENT AND REGROWTH

- There are many things in your life that have been familiar for so long, is hard to believe they can be replaced.

- It was extremely difficult to replace friends, habits, interests and desires but in order to progress somethings have to be replaced or cut so they can re-grow in the right direction.

- Sometimes a tree branch is cut off so it can be replaced with a new one that grows in the right direction where the previous one had grown in the wrong direction.

- When one wants to lose weight bad foods have to be replaced by good foods. Some things in your life that you love or were accustomed to have to be replaced in order for you to live and achieve your full potential

- Replacement is never easy but is necessary.

CHAPTER 10

THE LIFE....

My second year of College was again a period of testing and growth. I returned to ORU and was faced with new challenges. During the summer I had spent time working with my Church's youth group, witnessing on the streets wherever I could, growing in the Lord and enjoying life. I learned the art of hanging out by myself. I spent time reading Christian books and listening to teaching tapes and CHRISTIAN MUSIC, jogging, playing basketball, swimming and enjoying the simple things of life in a way I had never done before.

I had become active in my Church's youth ministry, but still felt uncomfortable around the Church crew. I knew I should be in Church and I knew the Bible said not to forsake the assembly of ourselves with others, so I stuck with it. There were good periods and bad periods with the Church. The Youth Pastor was a very likeable guy and he did many innovative and creative things to stimulate my interest. I did enjoy being around the Church, but it was just that they were from such a different background.

Returning to College this time was different. My brother-in-law and sister had moved to Charlotte North Carolina and my girlfriend during my second year of College, who was a Christian had moved back home. I felt almost as strange as I did during my first year, but I was always the type who could function alone almost anywhere in the world.

Without my previous spiritual big brother and sister, I had to deal with the challenges of College life on my own. I basically dealt with it by focusing on my books, playing ball and more books. I did not have any real friends at this time although there were acquaintances. I lived in my own world. I didn't go to Church as often as I did previously, but I still read my Bible and prayed.

Things changed significantly after the first semester of my second year. I had a new roommate and I met a young lady and we became friends. It was also during this time that I became friends with another gentleman, who would be my best friend in College.

My third year was a time when I developed a number of friends that I didn't have before. It seems that most of my friendships in life had started out in an adversarial role. I was playing basketball and we ended up tangling and pushing each other exchanging words on the court. It was nothing unusual, just some hard basketball and it was not like we were going to fight or anything.

After a while, a guy named Mike Hairston and I became a really good friends and most of the time we hung together. He was a long distance runner and also a pretty good basketball player. We used to run together a lot and play basketball. We had many one-on-one duels and we played on the same team many times.

Later on, there was another group of friends that I got together with who formed our team. Several of us used to hang together and have a good time. I also started a team that played in the school's intra-mural league. I named the team the Underground.

It consisted of Jeff Lee, Lance Harris, Carl Livingston and a few others. Our team was mostly Black players and ORU was predominantly White. We didn't have any racial issues, but we had put a team together that was from the "Hood," as you would say. We beat a lot of teams and even went to the playoffs. We had a good time playing together and fellowshipping. I did get in one problem where I got angry with the Referee and picked up a volleyball pole and went after him with it. Fortunately it did not end up too badly; I had to apologize and meet with the Dean of men. It was not until years later that I realized that one of the black brothers in the administration we referred to as Bobo had saved me from being thrown out of school.

During that year I had two or three female friends. One was Debbie, a beauty queen and singer with the Oral Roberts Ministries. We had some good times talking and going out to dinner, movies and just chilling. I learned a lot about relating to ladies on the friendship level, as opposed to the way I had done things before. I really did not concentrate on "love" relationships. For the first time, I had learned how to have a clean friendship relationship with the opposite sex.

After a fruitful year and a half, it was time for me to graduate. I had a lot more friends than I did when I first arrived. In fact, all the guys, Jeff Lee, Lance, Mike and the others were trying to convince me to come back for the Fall Semester instead of completing my education during the summer months. I decided to finish up during the summer, because I was ready to move on with life. I felt my mission was accomplished at ORU, I had learned to be a much better person; I received an education and learned how to relate better to the opposite sex.

After that summer, it was time to face the world. I had offers to stay in Tulsa and work but the more I thought about it, the more

I felt like going home. Something inside of me said why spend your time reaching young people in a land far away in a different culture when you left behind thousands of young people you know and have access to.

I had begun working with Youth for Christ in Tulsa, Oklahoma overseeing camps and special programs for juvenile delinquents. After considering the offer from Youth for Christ, in the end I decided it was time to return to my roots and see what the Lord had in store for me.

Before I returned home, I decided I needed to chill for a while, so I did as I normally did during my school years at ORU; I went to Charlotte North Carolina, where Robyn and Marilyn were pastors, to just relax and kick back before heading back to Nassau. For about a month I just chilled, read my Bible, played some hoops and listened to the voice of the Lord. The more I listened for that still small voice, the more I kept hearing, "Return home." Robyn had kept an invitation open for me to work with him if I did not return home, but I decided to return home, as this seemed to be the direction of the Lord.

One of the more important and strategic meetings of my life up to that point was while I was still at ORU. During my early teens I had heard of Myles Monroe and his band of musicians called the Visionaries. They began in the early Seventies and caused major stirrings in the Bahamas when they took the popular music style of the day and went about reaching the youth with the funky sounds of the Seventies.

All over the Bahamas, there was talk about Myles Munroe and the Visionaries and what he was doing with music. The young people loved it, some Church people cautioned him, and others let him know he was of the devil. As a teenager, I was not into Christian music or gospel music so our paths never crossed although my sisters knew him well. They actually worked along with him at Crusades and concerts and spoke very well of him. There was even a time when he came to my high school and a number of students got saved. I walked outside before the concert was finished because I did not want to be confronted with Gospel. Other than what I had heard, I did not know him.

I don't remember the exact reason or time, but we met and talked and I remember that the conversation was one of encouragement for me to be the best that I could be. We initially were never really close at ORU, but we got to know each other and developed a friendship. I was not quite fully integrated into the deep spiritual world he was in, and I was hanging around with some of the athletes who were not known to be really spiritual. I was into some different things, but something clicked and we continued to communicate on and off. I remember Myles encouraging me to attend the small Chapel Services that included Communion a few times each week. This proved to be a wonderful spiritual experience for me, and allowed me to reflect on my life and how I was progressing as a Christian. Myles had encouraged me in many ways and this relationship would prove instrumental in my future development as a Christian and Leader.

LESSON #10
ENJOY THE MOMENT

- Life was meant to be enjoyed, so many people postpone enjoying life until things get better.

- Because tomorrow is not guaranteed, enjoy today and make the most of every opportunity.

- Always celebrate the special moments of life, every victory no matter how small, every fruitful relationship no matter how short.

- Fun is completely necessary and we should have fun, but fun should never kill you or endanger your well being.

- It is possible to have fun without intoxication, evil and treachery.

- Pleasure is apart of our purpose but pleasure is meant for the right moments and circumstances. Pleasure outside of purpose becomes abuse.

CHAPTER 11

TOO FAR GONE

As I returned home from Charlotte, North Carolina, the best way I could describe myself was too far gone. It was like I was in a zone. I knew that there was no turning back. In fact I had become a rebel with a different cause. I was committed to my new life, and what I had experienced had convinced me that I had discovered the true meaning and purpose of life.

I read books weekly, listened to tapes, shared my testimony and experiences at every opportunity, and listened to Christian music exclusively for the first time in my life. I did not like the typical Church music, but I found Gospel R&B and Rock music, and this was a big help to me because I was a music freak. I also volunteered to help the youth pastor and the pastor of my Church. I was happy to help them and to inspire younger persons to seek what I had found in Christ.

Not contented to just wait for things to happen, I began to conduct my own Bible studies with young people from my Church and with family members and friends from my old neighborhood. I still loved sports and would frequent local parks where I played pick-up basketball, and with local teams in what is known as the government league. I jogged and ran in road races with my younger brother, Congo Bill, who was a track athlete with the Bain Town Flyers. I did whatever I could to witness and encourage others.

I taught Sunday school and assisted with Youth Meetings. I was motivated by my commitment to the life changing power of Christ. I played ball on the courts, where people would be cussing and I wore my witness T-shirts. Many times guys on the park would be smoking weed or being obscene and they noticed I wouldn't join them, so they would ask me questions about why I was different. Eventually many of them showed respect for me and would even stop cursing when I was around.

This was a new life and I was enjoying every minute of it. I knew I would not turn back because I was just too far gone. At other times, I returned to the streets where I grew up and hung out with guys who were using drugs, cussing and fighting but I only hung out to share the Word, I never became like them. It was odd and awkward sometimes because some of my friends would ask me questions and some of them ridiculed my decision, as they said I would never make it because I was too bad. One thing I did notice is that whenever we were one-on-one, almost all of my "boys" would let me know they respected my decision though they were not prepared to follow me.

After a while of working with the Church where I grew up in, Myles Munroe returned to the Bahamas. I remembered what I had experienced while I was at ORU and it was a different kind of Church, so I was happy when he talked about introducing that type of worship in the Bahamas.

My previous experiences with Church had tainted my view. There were three types of Churches I remembered and I didn't like any of them. There was the traditional Anglican Church where I had grown up in, and I thought of their style of worship as being too dull. On the other, there was what appeared to be an emotional circus that we called the 'jumper Church,' which I was almost afraid of when growing up. Then there were the Churches in the middle that, again did not appeal to me. In most Churches I never saw strong men and hardly ever saw anyone from the streets, so I almost had the impression that Church was the domain of mostly older ladies and "soft" guys.

The Churches in Tulsa were much more to my liking; their music was contemporary, "funky", and something I could relate to. Their teachings were positive, focusing on the goodness of God and not the hardships or supposed hardships of the Christian life. This was the thing that really made a difference in my perception of Christianity. For the first time, I saw everyday people from all walks of life, who seemed excited about God and were not all waiting to escape and go to Heaven. I liked the fact that they spoke of "dominion" of having authority on earth and about God wanting us to have the good life or the "abundant" life.

When Myles Munroe returned home, we talked on and off about beginning a similar work in the Bahamas, because almost all Churches here were strict denominational affiliates, which could not change enough to deal with this 'new thing." Also, we both agreed that the existing Churches were not appealing to youth. Myles had the vision, I had the same idea in my mind, so we along with two others, Richard Pinder and Henry Francis, met and discussed the idea for a new type of Church; much like what I had become accustomed to. That decision ended up with the formation of Bahamas Faith Ministries (BFM).

BFM as it has been and is called, changed the face of the Bahamas. Dynamic praise and worship combined with teaching and a commitment to the power of the Holy Spirit in Today's world, resulted in scores of young and old coming to know the Lord and their lives being changed. Drug addicts, people of shady backgrounds, all came to the Lord through this ministry.

As time passed, I left my mother's Church and became fully involved in BFM. I left not because of any disagreement, but because I could see more clearly and identify more with what was taking shape at BFM than any other Church in the Bahamas. My commitment was strong. I drove the bus, worked in the tape ministry, taught Sunday school, picked up friends who were on drugs and worked with them; I spoke in schools, Churches, played ball and witnessed at every opportunity. I worked the book table, the tape ministry, went to prayer meetings, Fasted and lived according to the Word of God. I knew what I was doing was right and I continued to a point of no return.

Some people in life head in a certain direction and there comes a point in time when you would look at them and say they are too far gone. Well, I became one of those people.

From the time I committed my life to Jesus Christ, I knew that I had done the right thing. I went through difficult periods, through temptations and feelings of wanting to go back to what I came out of. Fortunately there came a point in time when I just knew without any doubt that I would not turn back. After years of living the word, dealing with the 'ins and outs' of life, I had come to the conclusion that if this is not it, then there is nothing else, and life makes no sense. I could not become convinced otherwise. I knew what happened to me, and I saw lives changed everyday, and nothing in this world I have seen parallels the power of God working in people's lives.

I have seen drug addicts completely changed, people who could not stay married changed, all manner of criminals and degenerates completely changed, because of one thing; their relationship with Jesus Christ.

My beliefs had become very serious. I looked at other religions and concluded that the Bible is true, "Jesus is THE way, The Truth and The Light" for me. I became convinced that God came into this world in the form of man to redeem mankind from his sin and separation from God. I have concluded that it is just that simple.

I had become like a crack addict, or a ninja soldier, addicted to and dedicated to living what I believed. At this point I was no longer a physically violent person, but I was still very much a rebel, still dedicated to this cause. This time my violence was at a higher level. I was fighting for the souls of young people. Those who are out there hurting, crying out for family, and crying out for direction in this confused and disoriented world.

I have made it my job to do as Jesus said, "Go into all the world and preach, teach and disciple." I did it at every opportunity, and while on the basketball court I would tell young people there is a better way; in the parks, I tell young people there is a better way… in the schools, Churches, on the streets or wherever I found myself. My message was the same. I was carrying bullets with me of a different kind. I carried tracts with a message of hope for this generation. I carried books; I held a microphone and would talk, some times I would even join the music and drop a few rhymes of my own, and I just could not stop and can't stop.

It's amazing to think about how I used to get high almost everyday, and now I have discovered a new high. No smoke involved, no powder, no pills; just pure Holy Spirit high or as I like to say, "I'm getting high strictly on the "Most High."

One of the amazing things I discovered about life in Christ is that you get some of the same feelings of being high as a Christian, as you did on drugs. No joke. Sometimes when I would jam praise and worship music and worship the Lord and pray, I could swear I just lit up a big joint. But it's different now, no hangover, no feeling of depression afterwards, just pure Holy Spirit.

In this world, life and death has become a day-to-day challenge. Bullets can separate any of us from life in an instant. We live in a jungle in many ways. But I realize this is exactly what the Bible said life would come to. So I live like I am in a war zone because I am. I don't wait to be shot and I don't wait for the fight to come to me. I realize the times we are living in and I fire my own shots. I am not ashamed of the Gospel; truth is truth and if someone can't deal with the truth that I'm sharing, I have to do what Jesus said and keep walking.

LESSON #11
STICK WITH A GOOD THING

- Sometime it amazes me how people can achieve fulfillment and success only to abandon it for more unfavourable circumstances.
- If you have found peace, stability or success, stay with the winning formula.
- Learn to enjoy the benefits of a good decision. Build on success by not altering what got you to the point of success.
- As long are you are winning there is no need to change
- If you relied on God for success why abandon him when you get there.

CHAPTER 12

WHAT ABOUT YOUR FRIENDS?

Yeah what about my friends? The story of my friends is a story of tragedy. I wish I could offer hope and inspiration from what happened to them and me since we parted ways, but unfortunately the story does not end that way. I'm sure this story is repeated around the world, especially in Black communities from the ghettos of the USA to the underground in Jamaica and to the Black neighborhoods of London.

MY FRIENDS

SQ.... is married and living between another Caribbean country and the United States. Several years ago he was shot by a policeman in a dispute, but seems to be doing okay. He seemed to settle down, but I remember receiving a call from one of his relatives, who asked me to talk to him because he was becoming violent and using alcohol and drugs. Since that time, things may have gotten better but I can't say for sure. I will never forget how his relative called and said Mr. Burrows I don't know you he talked about you and how you changed your life so I decided to call because he respects you.

DCT – Has worked a number of jobs, dealing cocaine for a

while, hustling on the streets and working various jobs; still into girls, but does not seem to be making much progress. I seldom see him, but it didn't seem like he was headed in the right direction.

Skeeter – After high school we separated, he became a serious drug addict. After some serious situations that almost cost his life, his eyes opened and he went into rehabilitation. For sometime he was a recovering drug addict. Later he turned his life around and worked as a carpenter. He died but thank God he had recovered. I believe he had made a commitment to Christ and was working with his Church when he died. I remember him telling me over and over that he could not believe I had actually made it as a Christian. He said after he saw me make it, he realized he could too.

DI – He learned to slide between the world of drug dealing and business. He ended up like most of my friends with a severe cocaine addiction, eventually recovering and seeming to overcome those past demons. He and my brother went back into drug dealing for a while but eventually he got out of it. He seems to have survived as a businessman and had several businesses. He ended up getting married for the second or third time and is doing his best to make it.

The Pimp – Has struggled with alcoholic and drug addictions, while working in the entertainment industry. He was still working in his field and battling with life's issues. He showed a lot of potential, but substance abuse stunted his growth and he still seems to be plagued by the same issues.

Rev – I remember he used to come on the block after Church and always had money to gamble with. His father pastored a Church, and though we called him Rev, he was no real Rev. by a long shot. A few years after I had gotten saved I saw him and he told me how he had gotten stabbed by another one of my old friends. The next time I saw him he was on cocaine and in bad shape. As of this writing I'm not sure if he has overcome his cocaine addiction or not.

KX – One of my few friends who got married early on. Although he got married I am not sure if he was ever really faithful to his wife. He liked to party and loved women. He also had bouts with cocaine. To this day, I think he is still a party man and I'm not really sure if he is completely stable.

TW – He was so instrumental in getting me into drugs and some of the negative aspects of life I never knew had stints in prison; became a cocaine addict for many years and has struggled to keep his life together. He went to prison and was in and out of trouble for a while. He seems to have left the ways of the street and has been trying hard to work in the business world and stay away from criminal activities. He did get married and seemed to have stabilized his life, but it's hard to say for sure.

Priest – He died of an overdose of cocaine. Since we parted ways, he was shot during a drug deal, overdosed several times, and stayed in and out of trouble. My final conversation with him was a reflection of someone who was searching but could not commit himself to find the truth. After his first overdose when he was run down by two cars and suffered numerous internal injuries including a collapsed lung, he said these words to me when I invited him to Church, "Davy B, you are doing a good thing, one of these days I will join you, but I'm not ready yet"....I wish he was ready and I hope he had time to make himself ready because less than a year later he was dead.

GF – The last time I saw him, he was a crack addict, living on the streets, in and out of trouble with the law, and living as life comes. At times he has looked really bad like most crack heads do, so it seems like his life has not been going well. Hopefully it's gotten better, but it does not seem so.

BC – I spoke with him when he first went to jail for armed robbery. He said he would not go back and that he had changed. He was not ready for the Christian "stuff," as he put it. A few years later he was in the hospital after being beaten by a gang. He only had one intention, to get out of the hospital and get back at the guys who attacked him. As I listened to the news a few years later, I heard the story about how he murdered another young man over drugs, and shot him with a shotgun. He was sentenced to death. The sentence was never carried out, so he remains on death row in prison for life.

KT – Although he had opportunities for a good education, he chose to stay on the street. He adopted the Rastafarian lifestyle while dealing cocaine and weed. At our last conversation, he still lived the same way although he had gotten married and had several children.

BST – I listened to the news and noted that he was charged with attempted murder. Later as I picked him up, he explained his innocence. He eventually won his case. All he wanted from me at the time was a few dollars. He did not want to let me know he was still a cocaine addict, but I could see it all over him. We talked about old times, but I was sad to see his state of mind. I asked him to come and see me and he did. We talked about him giving his life to God as I did, and he said he would think about it, but I did not see him again after that. He said he might come to Church, but he never came. A few years later, I picked up the newspaper and saw his photo in the obituary column. I didn't even know he had died. I went to the funeral and sat in the back. It was a really sad occasion for me. I didn't see any of our old friends we used to hang with. I sat there and cried; he died of AIDS.

BB – Had some difficulties and spent a period of time as a cocaine addict, but he recovered, got married and has had decent jobs. He had his battles with cocaine, but now seems to be over it. He does not attend Church to my knowledge and seems to have toned down the violence he was famous for. He has had a decent job for a long time in his profession and from that stand point he seems to be doing okay.

FG – Graduated from college and got a decent job, but he got hooked on cocaine and has never fully recovered. He has been through six or seven rehabilitation programs, but seems to always fall back into the cocaine trip. One day he stopped me and asked me what was it I had, which helped me to get away from the life I lived. We talked and I told him that the reason for my success was my relationship with the Lord and that I had given my life to Christ, and my life had been changed because of this. He made a commitment to Christ and has tried real hard, but has not seemed to have been able to conquer his drug habit.

007 – Several years ago I was told he got shot in his side during an incident outside a local nightclub. He later spent a number of years as a cocaine addict, but came to Church, gave his life to the Lord and seemed to be doing well. Unfortunately I was told that he was involved in domestic issues with his girlfriend; he went back on drugs and has never fully recovered. At last report, he was doing better, but still going through the challenges of life.

NP – Amazing that he is still alive. He was an alcoholic, drug addict, who went to prison. He went through many violent episodes and through so many rough experiences in life I always wondered how he stayed alive. The last time I checked he was trying his best but had gotten very sick and was somewhat incapacitated.

PB – After I gave my life to the Lord, he went to live in the USA for a time. He worked on a horse farm for thoroughbreds and did some drugs on the side for recreation. Later he returned home and was re-involved in the drug trade, dealing with the Cuban Mafia and local drug dealers, including police officers on the take. After finding out about him still being involved in the drug trade, I questioned him but he did not immediately change. We lived in the same house and he would see me reading my Bible, praying and listening to Christian music and teaching tapes. After some time of watching my lifestyle and actions, he eventually gave his life to the Lord. Today he is a devoted Christian, married with children and runs a successful business operation.

What I have noted in these cases is that this represents a limited sample of my friends from the past. The way their lives have gone is a testimony to the value of my commitment to the Lord. These are just some of my friends. There are many others, who I can mention but as you can see my friends and I took a mostly very different course. Some have been and are still in prison for years; some died violent deaths and others, who are very few in numbers, made the change and lived productive lives. The main difference between my friends and me was my key decision to submit my life to Christ. The lesson I believe should be obvious.

LESSON #12

- Success is not success if you have no one to share it with

- When you help others get to their destiny you will always experience unexpected rewards

- Because we were not designed to be alone, find someone who needs to go where you are going and your journey is much more enjoyable.

- When you help others you inspire yourself

- One of the greatest joys one can achieve is observing someone become what they were destined to be.

CHAPTER 13

RIGHTEOUS REBEL

After I came to Christ and changed my life, I felt it was my obligation to help others, especially young men from the background I came from. I realized that the Church was not an appealing place for many young men, but I also realized that it was the only hope for them and me. I discovered that hope, but they had not, so I made it my mission to execute the revolution of positive change. I wanted to use the same passion I had on the street to spread the Word of God and help rescue those I saw following the path of my friends and me. This part of the story chronicles my rise from the ashes of bad decisions and mishaps to where I am today as a hard core righteous rebel.

When I returned to the Bahamas, the first thing I did was connect with the Church that I grew up in and where my mother and sisters attended. I was welcomed with open arms by the Pastor and Youth Pastor and shared my testimony with them. After a period of acclimation, I began by teaching Sunday school and working with the youth group at Evangelistic Temple Assemblies of God Church.

I was dedicated and excited to be on the "other side" with my new found faith. I worked hard with the Church and did what I could to witness to others including friends from the old "hood." I picked up friends in the ghetto and brought them to Church, or took them with me when I was running errands for the Church. Some of them actually made commitments and got "saved," but most never stayed very long. It seems almost impossible for most of the guys from the street to turn things around and remain committed to Christ. Many days you could find me talking to hardcore street guys, who at the time were on cocaine and alcohol and losing jobs or family. I was just trying to get my friends to see the light.

During this period, I also worked with Youth for Christ for a period of time putting together programs and events to reach our youth. At that time, Youth for Christ was headed by "Stunce" Willams, who pioneered several new programs for youth and hosted some of the first Christian Television shows addressing youth matters. Things were going well in my work with the Church, I was having an impact on many young people to the point where I had started a home Bible study and personally taught Bible lessons to other young people and one or two friends from the street.

Things were going well and I was enjoying the ministry, but the traditional Church was still a challenge for me in some ways because I had been exposed to a more contemporary style and message while in Tulsa Oklahoma. I had privately longed for something like what I had experienced in Tulsa when I was in College so when Dr. Myles Munroe came along and asked me to join him, I jumped on it. I was looking forward to that type of ministry. There was nothing wrong with Evangelistic Temple, but I was ready for an experience more relevant to me and my new walk of faith.

I was there at the beginning of what has become known as BFM as the youngest member of its original Board. I sat in the living room of Pastor Henry Francis as Dr. Munroe, Dr. Richard Pinder, Pas. Henry Francis and I put together a new entity called Bahamas Faith Ministries. This new ministry was totally different from other Churches in the Bahamas at that time, as it was designed to be more than a Church. From the beginning, Myles Munroe had a world vision far beyond the traditional Church concept.

I dedicated my life to this new Church even when it meant I had to miss a playoff basketball game for one of my teams. I can remember my team mates pleading with me to come to a game, but I told them I had to go to Church. I felt bad at the time and even worse when I looked back at it, but I had made God my first priority and though I loved basketball, it came second.

At this same time, I was employed by the Ministry of Youth, putting together programs for the Ministry for school students, young business persons and more. I was founding director of a unit called the Small Business Center, and put together a conference each year for new business persons under the age of 25 called the "Youth in Business Expo."

I had a very successful time at the Ministry of Youth working with schools and business people, while working on a volunteer basis in Youth Ministry. My time there developed into controversy, as I had a difficult time relating to the traditional Church and began hitting the streets spreading the "Good News." My approach revolutionized Youth Ministry in the Bahamas and in many areas of the world, as I developed street outreaches and introduced Gospel Reggae and Rap/Hip Hop during street and community outreaches. These outreaches impacted the local gang scene and saw hundreds of young men commit their lives to Christ. It was during this time that some of the young men I worked with bestowed upon me the nickname of the "Ruffneck" Pastor, a name that stuck for years and struck a chord among disenfranchised youth, as well as the community at large.

Those years were interesting to say the least. At times I would be on the basketball court playing with guys who had guns in their waists, witnessing brutal fights that caused some of my Christian friends, who had not grown up on the streets, to panic. I told them to stay calm and only panic if they heard gunshots. They were asking, "...you sure? I realized that these guys who were fighting had no beefs with us, so they would not harm us intentionally. Actually I went into some of the areas, and they would come up and talk to me, so the younger guys respected me. Many schools and communities called on me to work with young men at that time and they appreciated the impact I was having on them.

A few years later I was joined by a former drug dealer and gang banger, Carlos Reid and together we launched an initiative called "Peace on the Streets" as a response to the growing violence in the inner city. A mutual friend introduced Carlos to me, because he said Carlos was from a similar background and he felt we could work together to help save a lot of young men.

Carlos and I got together and began doing street outreaches, park outreaches and school outreaches. We solicited the help of a variety of other young men from street backgrounds, including former drug addicts, criminals and gangbangers. We called this group "The Crew." The Crew was everywhere at that time. We had a major impact on the streets to the point where policemen would ask us to please go into some of the violent communities and do an outreach, because when we did outreaches, violence would decline in those areas. We were in the news because this outreach lasted over two years and we saw over 1,000 gang members make commitments to Christ.

During this period we held major youth events and outreaches that attracted thousands of youth, leading many to change their course in life. At one point, we were picking up bus loads of gang bangers from areas in the ghetto. Some of the young men were from the "The Border Boys," "East Street Rebellions," "Bain Town Gun Dogs," and "Nassau Village Rebellions" as well as many others.

These young men came to Church with guns in their waists and some ended up turning in their guns as they dedicated their lives to Christ. Most of the young men unfortunately returned to the streets, but in the next chapter, I will chronicle some of their successes.

In addition to Peace on the Streets, along with Dr. Myles Munroe I launched a number of successful events and programs including an annual youth Conference titled Youth Alive that has attracted almost 7,000 teens over a six day period. Some nights, Youth Alive attracted almost 3,000 teens. We used drama, music, video and sound to creatively present the Gospel to the youth. We also held revolutionary parties that had all the trappings of regular parties, but without the alcohol and lewd behavior. These parties changed the thinking of youth about having clean fun in a Christian setting.

I was also able to establish the Christian Youth Talent Jam, which launched the careers of most of the popular young artists in the Bahamas. Persons who became recording artists, such as Landlord, Selector, Monty G, Marky Maxx, DJ Counsellor, Ta Da, and others all were products of our Talent Jam.

This was the one event that teens could look forward to that focused on clean positive talent. The list of those who came from talent jam is legendary in Bahamian circles. System 3, Selector, Christian Massive, Monty G, , Landlord, Mr. Lynx, DJ Counsellor, Ta DA, Supernatural, Double Syxx, Manifest and Dunamus, Syntist and many more.

Our youth ministry was first called Live Youth and featured a lively and aggressive group of young people who were revolutionizing Nassau. Live Youth was the birthplace of the first travelling Christian rap group from the Bahamas called System 3, who toured the world pioneering Caribbean Gospel Hip Hop and Rap consisting of Kevin Harris, Delano Johnson and Antonio "Tones" Thompson. System 3 traversed the Caribbean and USA and was nominated to receive a Grammy award as part of a Motown Gospel Song featuring Stevie Wonder and other popular secular artists.

After changing the name to Youth Alive, we continued to trail blaze the youth ministry, and we featured another event called Operation Burnout, which was an all night affair featuring games, music and clean fun along with spiritual instruction. We also launched Boat cruises, and pioneered radio and TV programs for youth, that were truly youth oriented and challenged many of the existing conventions.

I would be the first to say that I made some mistakes along the way, and at times I was too unconventional, but my passion to reach young people was my motivation and God worked with me every step of the way to refine my issues. I was probably the first Pastor to take Reggae and rap artists into schools and neighborhoods and this created a real stir in the Church world. Many Churches even began preaching against me, though I was reaching youth in large numbers, they were coming to Christ and impacting their neighborhoods and schools.

In the 1990's, I introduced the first Holy Hip Hop event that saw over 300 gang members come to Christ and resulted in the formation of a group of former gang members, who came to be known as Christian Massive. We did many things for the Bahamas youth ministry that were new to the Bahamas. I was simply trying to do what Jesus said. He said we are to go into all the world and preach the Gospel and I happened to believe that meant the world of youth.

Too often the Church asked us to reach youth, but would do nothing to understand and appreciate the culture of youth. We had fun events and parties that defied traditional logic, because it was considered to be too much fun. We worked with a Christian DJ known as Brother Vic. to stage these parties that consisted of clean Gospel Reggae and hip hop and dances with no vulgarity, no alcohol and overt Christian messages. We also took our parties to the seas in the form of boat cruises that had a similar format. Many young people saw this as a new hope and they felt they could finally enjoy themselves as Christians and still serve God fully.

Fortunately through the grace of God, we were able to help many young men and women turn their lives around. Some of these stories are illuminated later in this book. The programs we started have served as a model for youth ministry in the Bahamas and other areas of the world and we have received invitations from Churches, organizations, schools and other groups to conduct seminars on reaching youth.

The work of Youth Alive and Peace on the Streets attracted the attention of the Minister of Youth and The Prime Minister of the Bahamas, who invited the Peace on the Street team to the

Cabinet office to offer assistance after recognizing the impact of the program. Eventually the government threw its support behind the initiative and helped establish "Operation Redemption" a car wash and maintenance program that allowed former gang members to earn a living and become prepared to reenter society.

At that time, Dr. Munroe had begun having an impact on the international scene and he began publishing books. With his encouragement, I was inspired to begin writing books directed at youth as he was doing with adults. From this, I was able to write and publish many books, and I traveled to many areas of the United States, Canada and the Caribbean, as an inspirational and motivational speaker for Church events, government sponsored events, school assemblies and outreaches. Churches began to call on me and entire denominations that had once considered me as an evil person; began to invite me, because they saw so many of their young people become a part and get involved; as they were inspired by what we were doing. In the later years, we developed a program called, "Strictly Positive Tour" that has gone into schools and communities with a combination of positive music, drama and messages that have inspired thousands of youth to commit to Christ.

I continued in Ministry and have been blessed with a wonderful wife, Angela, who has stood beside me and supported me at every turn. I could not be where I am today without the support I received from her. She has ministered alongside me and has established her own ministry to young ladies over the years. My two children have also served with me and supported me in Ministry since they were toddlers. Davrielle and Arri could always be seen with me every step of the way through every event. Davy B, the Rebel and bad boy, had come home and returned as a Righteous Rebel.

CHAPTER 14

CHANGE IS POSSIBLE.... YOUNG REBELS OF TODAY

My story is one of the millions that have occurred for years among our youth. The things I did and the life I lived happened many years ago. As we look around our society today, the natural question is what is going on? Are there others like me who walked the streets, lived as young rebels, but have made a change? The answer is yes, and listed below are stories about a few other young rebels who made a positive change.

The stories have changed, the faces have changed but the beat goes on. I realized just how much time had changed the other day, when I went to play basketball and one of the guys was playing with a gun in his waist, and another guy had a knife in his waist on the neighborhood basketball park. In spite of this violent and misguided world that we live in, these young men have managed to escape and turn their lives around through the same process of hope, purpose and commitment to Christ.

Selector – As a young man, Selector got involved in drugs and gang activity, encountered scrapes with the law for robbery and other criminal matters. At one time, he went into a Church Service and robbed the congregation. During one of our Peace on the Street events, he gave his life to Christ, gave up drugs; he became interested in learning about sound production and performing as a singer. Today Selector has recorded several albums. He works full time for the Church as a sound engineer, and has established his own sound company. Although he never graduated from high school, he taught himself through courses on the internet on how to do music mastering and is one of only a few Bahamians who is accomplished in mastering music. He is also married today and has three children.

Landlord (Orlando Miller) – Had a rough life and he did not know who his father was and his mother had many personal challenges, so he ended up as a young gang member sometimes sleeping in cars and surviving on his own. During another one of our "Peace on the Streets" events, he gave his life to the Lord and started working to become a better person. I honestly didn't think he would make it at first, because it seemed we had forced him to become a Christian with so many members of the Peace on the Street guys telling him he had to "get saved." Today Landlord has moved from being a gang banger to a businessman and recording artist. His music has been featured on Caribbean MTV (Tempo), in Europe and on TBN and he has traveled extensively on his own doing his music and sometimes he travels with Dr. Myles Munroe, our senior pastor. He owns his own business (several Car Washes) and is married.

Raymond (Double Syxx) Eneas – Raymond came off of the streets and gave his life to Christ. Many of his friends ended up dead like mine, but today he is also a recording artist, a Youth Pastor and Businessman, and graduated from College with a degree in computer engineering. The amazing thing about Raymond's life story is that when he committed his life to Christ, truly incredible things began happening for him. He got a very good job at the Atlantis Resort, that is a world famous hotel in the Bahamas, but through involvement with our youth ministry and the Church his eyes began to open and he made the decision to go to college. He sometimes traveled with me on a ministry trip and incredible things happened on one of the trips. He met a lady who became like a second mother to him, and she assisted him with housing so he could go to college. On another occasion while travelling with me, he was introduced to his wife. Raymond earned a college degree in computer science and is a youth pastor in Florida, working on the completion of a Master's degree and owns a few businesses. He married the former Miss Florida Panhandle, who herself has a Master's degree and is an accomplished speaker and businesswoman.

Manifest – A young man who came into contact with us after being a secular DJ, who at one time was the DJ for gang events with the Rebellion gang. Beginning as a secular hip hop artist, he dedicated his life to Christ and decided to use his gift to glorify God. Today he is also married, owns his own business and is a gospel hip hop recording artist and owns a recording studio.

Jawarra – Came into the ministry after being a rebellious youth at one point having to sleep in the bushes to avoid gunmen who were out to kill him. Today he is one of my assistants in youth ministry, and is also married and has a family. He came to our youth ministry and dedicated his life to Christ. He travelled with us to an event hosted by one of my friends and a friend of Dr. Munroe named Ron Luce. The event is called "Acquire the Fire" hosted by Teen Mania. It was at this event that Jawarra was inspired and decided to attend the Honors Academy and began training as a youth leader. He returned home and later married my secretary, Ranel Hanna. Today they are working in various aspects of ministry.

Lorenzo – Was one of the young men I worked with at a school called HO Nash. He was a troubled gang member, who terrorized his school and did many horrible acts as a part of the Dogs gang. He gave his life to Christ and did well for a time before making a mistake and being charged with attempted murder. He was able to recover from this mistake and is today working in ministry with his Church.

Kent "Spy" Johnson – Was another young man who grew up on the streets as a young drug dealer and gang banger. He terrorized many in Nassau's Yellow Elder community. He ended up giving his life to Christ and became a part of the Youth Alive outreaches, where many gang members came to know Christ. His musical talent came to the forefront at that time, as he was one of the early winners of our Talent Jam and he began using his talents to impact other teens as the founding leader of a group known as "Christian Massive." "Spy" later became an integral part of our Peace on the Street Campaign and continues today in spite of many challenges and difficulties he faced along the way.

Franco – A young man whose parents were of Haitian decent, he became engulfed into the gang life at an early age. He also made a commitment to Christ and went on to Bible school at World Harvest Bible College in Ohio. He returned home and worked with a local Church as a Youth Pastor for a period of time before eventually launching out into ministry in the United States, where he continues in Ministry today.

There are many other success stories that I could share, but these stories are meant to encourage you and let younger persons know that all things are possible if they believe and turn from their evil ways. There are also many success stories about young ladies, but I have focused on the males, who have made it from the street and gang world, because many times young men tend to believe they can not make it in the "Kingdom of God." These stories prove that change is possible.

CHAPTER 15

MY WIFE AND KIDS

It's been a long and exciting journey to where I am today, and I thank God for where He has brought me from and where I am today. The person I am today is the fruit from seeds that were planted long ago. Although I did not take heed to the call initially, the many words that were spoken to me and over me, the prayers and intervention of people who care; all of these things helped me to become the person I am today.

One pivotal event in my life that has helped me in so many ways was finding the right mate. The Bible says the person who finds a wife finds a good thing and I must say that after wasting several years on women and drugs, I found out the true meaning of this verse. I cannot under-estimate the importance of waiting on God's timing and preparing for the right person.

I was busy serving God and doing my best to advance His Kingdom, and although I was always attracted to women and had female friends, there was a time when that was not my concentration. I was working "in the Kingdom." It is said that if you take care of God's business, He will take care of yours; so I guess as I tried to take care of God's business and developed myself, he took care of my need to have a good wife.

I was busy working with my Church and serving God when I went to Church one day and my cousin asked me a strange question. She had seen me with foreign women and a White missionary girl from the group, Youth With a Mission, so she asked why I wasn't interested in any Bahamian girls. As she was talking to me, Angie was standing by her and out of the blue I said I might be interested in your friend. I can't remember if she heard me but from that point on, we started talking.

Our first date was one of the most interesting encounters I had ever had with a female, but it told me a lot about Angie's qualities. I remember going to her house to pick her up and after opening my car door, I proceeded to get into the drivers seat and start the car. She just stood there by the passenger door and would not move. I wondered what was wrong with this girl, but I later realized she was waiting for me to be a gentleman and open the door for her. I got the message and that was the beginning of my retraining to become a real man. I got out and opened the door and we developed a friendship that was first about the "Word of God." We would spend many nights together studying the Bible and listening to tapes, going to the movies, dinners and special events. We attended the same Church and as I began ministry with Bahamas Faith Ministries, she joined me and served faithfully from the beginning.

My life was coming together and preparing me for a brand new journey. Angie decided to go to College at the same school I attended, so I was left at home continuing to do ministry with Dr. Myles Munroe and Bahamas Faith Ministries, while working full time with the Bahamas Ministry of Youth and Sports.

We stayed in touch during her college years and at times I would visit her, while staying with one of my friends, Mike Hairston or Ron Luce (who had just graduated from ORU), and we also enjoyed our time together.

Finally after three long years, Angie and I were married and the journey commenced. We grew together as a couple and went through the normal marriage challenges, but through it all we kept God's Word as our focus and we stayed true to the cause. We both serve in Ministry and are doing our best to help young people achieve their destiny.

Today we have two beautiful grown children, a son and daughter. Our son recently graduated from college and works for a successful accounting firm in New York, and our daughter is completing her first year at ORU. Both children grew up in the Ministry actively serving along with us in the Youth Ministry.

CHAPTER 16

WHERE IN THE WORLD IS DAVY B NOW?

It's been a long and exciting journey to where I am today, but I thank God for where he has brought me from. Today, I serve as president of three international organizations: The International Third World Youth Leaders Association, Global Youth Ministry Leadership Network and Youth Alive Ministries.

In addition to these international affiliations, I serve as Pastor of Totally Youth Church known as TYC, which is a very unique organization under the covering Ministry of Dr. Myles Munroe. This unique Church is an actual Church for teens. We conduct our own meetings and services and have pastors, leaders and workers, yet functioning along side the adult Church of Bahamas Faith Ministries International.

TYC is a Church for teens that has allowed for tremendous growth, innovation and impact, as teens are able to fully participate and serve in their own ministry. I have faithfully presided over this arrangement, and I have seen many young leaders develop and fulfil their potential, because they were given opportunities not normally afforded to youth.

Other Churches in the Bahamas are now following suit, and

I have travelled and shared this vision to help strengthen and recover today's youth and youth ministries in many cities and countries.

Prior to my present assignment, I worked for the Bahamas Government in the Ministry of Youth and Sports, where I orchestrated many highly successful programs for youth. Some of the programs included, "Youth in Business", "The Small Business Centre" which catered to young persons wanting to develop businesses; "Operation Experience" which allowed young persons to gain job experience during the summer months in fields of their choosing. During that time, I published mini booklets and magazines addressing issues such as Drug Abuse, Violence and Business.

Through the years I have been credited with revolutionizing youth ministry in the Bahamas and many areas of the world through a variety of unconventional programs that have impacted, gangs, drug users, troubled youth as well as everyday young people. For many years, my team members and I went to the streets and parks reaching out to youth who were troubled like me. As mentioned earlier, some of the methods I used were very unconventional for the Church, but it was these approaches such as using reggae music, rap and hip hop and drama that caused youth to believe I was down to earth (or down with them as they would say), and branded me with the nickname, "The Ruffneck Pastor."

I have had so many experiences in youth ministry that could become a volume of books. I can recall great successes and great challenges along the way. On one occasion one of the gang members I worked with was killed, in fact he was a gang leader who had changed his life. I had to preside over the funeral and in the graveyard we were surrounded by Policemen with Uzis and ak47s. At other times i have had to intervene and mediate, as gang members attempted to attack one of my youth. I ended up confronting the most vocal person and leader and reasoning with him and eventually convincing him that he needed to have some respect for the church. I also told him about my background and eventually was able to get him to leave without hurting the young man. Another time I had to intervene as one of my youth group members pulled a knife to stab another young man who had insulted me. He told the young man, "You don't insult my pastor. "The visitor ran outside and i ran behind them finally catching up with my youth group member and taking the knife from him.

Today I travel locally and internationally as a conference speaker motivating youth, Churches, youth ministries and school groups to maximize their God-given potential. I have had the good fortune of being a guest speaker and conducting seminars for many well known Churches and youth organizations including, Crenshaw Christian Center (Dr. Fredrick Price), and West Angeles Church of God in Christ (Bishop Charles Blake) in Los Angeles, California; Victory Christian Center (Pastor Robyn Gool) in North Carolina, Youth With a Mission, Youth for Christ, Christ For the Nations as well as Churches and conferences throughout the Caribbean, Europe and North America. I have also had the pleasure of working on programs in the Bahamas staged by Teen Mania, Promise Keepers and many others.

I am the author of nine books including Sex & Dating, Making the Most of Your Teenage Years, Strategies for Saving the Next Generation and Talk to Me, College Career and Money, Kingdom Parenting, What Do I Do Now and have hosted TV and radio programs including "The Ruffneck Myxx" and "Effective Youth", "The Youth and Family Show" and "Talk to Me". I have also had the pleasure of serving as executive producer of two sound tracks and four movies.

God has also blessed me to have appeared on many television and radio programs worldwide including programs hosted by TBN (Trinity Broadcasting Network), Richard Roberts (Hour of Healing) and TD Jakes (Potters Touch). I have also served as a contributing writer for many Christian Publications.

I have had the pleasure of serving as an advisor to the Bahamas Government on Youth Matters, having served three times as Chairman of the National Youth Advisory Council; a member of the Family Life and Health advisement group and the National Council on Drug Abuse. I founded programs for male mentorship "Young Champions", Christian School Clubs, "Christ 4 Life" and a young ladies mentorship program headed by my wife called "P31."

In addition to ministry work, the other side of my life has revolved around business; something that is a personal passion. I have enjoyed business since my early years of selling the wrong product on the streets to where I have started several businesses and two of them are currently thriving. I am blessed to be the owner and CEO of Megabyte Computers-a local computer company that specializes in hardware and software sales and supplies, and One Rib Publishing Company. One Rib Publications has grown from a small publishing company into a progressively developing media entity that continues to grow and impact both the local and international communities.

I am conducting many motivational and business and technology seminars for corporations, organizations and businesses. Several years ago I released a series entitled "Starting a Business and Maximizing Technology." I have also enjoyed my work as a motivational speaker, as President and CEO of the business and a motivational organization called "The Winners Touch."

My wife, Angela continues to minister along with me and runs the family businesses as a fulltime occupation allowing me to continue in ministry and travel. Our two beautiful children, Arri and Davrielle have inspired many other young people through their life example.

TYC and Youth Alive were both founded under the covering of Dr. Myles Munroe who has served as an inspirational mentor, advisor and in some ways as a big brother to me. His life example and encouragement has played a significant role in helping me to reach my destiny.

The things we do at Youth Alive and TYC are listed below with an overview of the extent of each work.

Youth Alive Ministries and TYC continue to impact youth offering a number of programs such as:

- Weekly: "Friday night live" fun, Bible teaching and youth training sessions.
- Monthly: "Super Sunday" youth spiritual growth meetings.
- "Stagez" - a program on Sunday mornings for teenagers, ages 13-15 and 16-19.
- Missions to various islands and countries as a group and in conjunction with Youth Missions organizations such as Teen Mania.
- Special conferences and events including, "OPERATION BURNOUT", "YOUTH ALIVE", and "CHRISTIAN YOUTH TALENT JAM".
- PROFESSIONAL YOUTH WORKSHOPS & SEMINARS such as , "Extreme Leadership", "Sex and Dating", "Conflict Resolution", "Parents & Teens", and "Strategies for Saving the next Generation", geared towards teens, parents, youth workers, pastors and young adults. These events involve drama, music and multimedia presentations.

- Drama, music and a variety of artistic expressions are shared as a means of sharing the gospel and providing alternatives for today's youth.
- Television shows "Talk 2 me" & "Effective Youth" & "Ruff-neck Myxx Video".
- Outreaches to schools, parks, streets, malls and foreign countries.
- Radio show "The Ruffneck Myxx".
- Concerts featuring contemporary Christian music artists.

Our work began as a local entity and has spread into many other countries.

EPILOGUE

The funny thing about this book is it that it's the first book that I had ever written, and after releasing eight books, I am finally releasing the first book that I wrote. I learned many lessons in my life, but the longer I live the more I realize the words of King Solomon in the Book of Ecclesiastes, where he says there is nothing new under the sun. Solomon also showed us through his life story that even the wise can go wrong if they choose not to follow the wisdom of God, but rather follow their own. I believe I qualify as Solomon did to comment on things I see behind me, ahead of me; things that are relevant to this world we live in and to the lives of our youth. With this thought in mind, I will call the thoughts that follow, 'A Word to the Wise.'

Solomon noted that there is nothing new under the sun and it seems that everything that happened before is happening again. I guess this will continue to happen. I predict that little will change as we look ahead. The pages of this book are a testimony as to what can and is going wrong in this world we live in among our youth. It is also a testimony of what can go right and how things can be turned around. But what I have learned over and over again is that change is often hard to face, especially when it means adults must face the music for things they did wrong and work with youth to change the future. How do I come to this conclusion?

First of all, a society or the world can only be as good as its families. No society can be successful without strong families.

So many of our youth grow up with no parents or in one parent homes, where that one parent is bearing a burden for the other parent, who is missing in action.

How can we talk about bringing the family back together when 60-70% of black families don't exist (no father, mother on crack, mother out hustling or prostituting, partying, father missing in action or abusive). When we have a family seminar and talk about what should be, what do we say to these youth who do not know what a family is? What do we say about what a father should be, where do they fit in when many young people are growing up with a negative connotation of the word 'father' itself because of their experiences.

There is really not much hope for total redemption in our society, because so many parents and youth are already damaged that Humpty Dumpty would be a minor problem in comparison. Many can be saved but I do not believe we can save most, because of the foundational problems already existing. What do I mean? First, we refuse to admit our own problems. We tell teenagers not to smoke weed (marijuana, herb) nor become involved in drugs, but we drink and promote beer and other kinds of alcohol. Who are we fooling and do we think they will listen to this hypocrisy? I can tell you that they won't. If adults cannot face the drugs they are using, do you think the youth will?

The way things are going right now, my advice is almost to build bigger jails, prepare for new levels of violence, and prepare for the return of the Wild, Wild West, where any gun can play.

We are living in a world where our parents cannot stay married to one another, cannot even trust one another, commit adultery on a regular basis, live dishonestly and then expect their children to grow up with morals and principles. Our political and Church leaders are often caught in dishonest activity, from adultery to bribery and more. Things will not get better the way we are going right now. Your children will be just like you and in most cases worse.

We talk about controlling guns but there are already too many guns on the street, you can get a gun like you can find water. The sad fact is that many of our youth cannot live without a gun, because even if they are not into something wrong they need one to try to survive in a world where so many of their peers have one and are prepared to use it at the slightest provocation.

Finally I believe that the truth is the truth and for what I can see, the truth is not being told. So many have said simple things like we need to go back to the Bible, way but in our world when one suggests the Bible as a reasonable standard, the "smart" people in society jump all over you for being old fashioned, and they try to solve our problems with new ideas.

In spite of the fact that even nature tells us that men and women are made for different purposes, we try to make ourselves believe that they are the same. Men cannot have children. They have different hormonal and physical makeup than women yet, we come up with "new" theories that say it is natural for two men to have a family together. This will never work. It cannot. The only result will be mixed up and confused children, who will take out their frustrations on us.

Like Solomon said all is vanity. The one purpose of man is to serve his creator. Everything else will be proven wrong. The designs of man will always fail until his designs are set to fit into the Master's plan. I cannot see how we can ignore the Maker or Manufacturer's instructions and still expect our product to properly work. The Bible states that if you want to see a good life and long days then go back to God. His plan for us through Him becoming human and sacrificing His life for us is what is stated in the Bible. So am I giving up?

No I'm not giving up, but to be honest with you I have to take the approach I heard in a story sometime ago. There were some men walking along the shore, and as they walked, they noticed that there were thousands of starfish in the sand away from the water. The star fish had been dragged onto the shore by some freak of nature and could not get back into the water. One of the men looked at the situation and hopelessly remarked that there were two many star fish for just the two of them to save by throwing them back in the water. It would take days to get all of the starfish back in the water. So he walked on and sadly said to his friend, we can't save them, they will all die. The other friend looked at him and agreed that all could not be saved, but he said to his friend while he picked up one of the star fish and threw it back in the water, "All of them can't make it, but this one will", then he picked up another one and said, "This one will make it too."

Today our young people are like those star fish, we can't save all, but there are some we can still reach and throw back in the water so they can live. I choose to keep working to save those I can, while realizing that many will not make it. Please join me.

Family photos

Dave's father: Leclain L. Burrows
(first black Bahamian private pilot,
entrepreneur, soldier in World War II)

"UNIVERSITY ON THE BLOCKS" – A group of youths in the Gambier constituency – Oakes Field area – recently came together and formed what they called and advertised by a huge sign at the junction of Warren Street and Hawthorne Road as "The University of Warren Street." A spokesman for the group seated with some of his colleagues pictured above on a wooden plant supported by concrete blocks, the only seat at the "University" told *The Guardian* Monday that they gathered to "rap" together. Among the topics during these "rapping" sessions which are conducted "anytime," day or night, are independence and the social disorders of Gambier constituency and the community. All "brothers on the block" become members of the "University" whose president was said to be Chimmy B., with Nippo Valentio as vice president and Boston Adderley as secretary. Qualifications necessary to gain admission to the "University" were cited as being a brother of the block and having an unemployment status.

The University of Warrant Street.

Highschool Basketball Team

Made in the USA
Columbia, SC
22 July 2025

60900048R00085